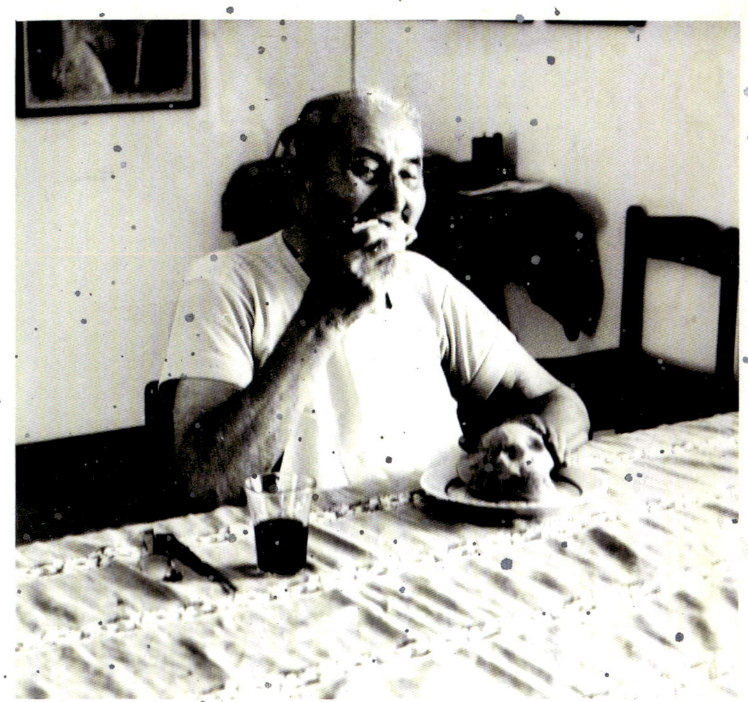

Pietro Roccasalva

GAMeC – Galleria d'Arte Moderna e Contemporanea di Bergamo

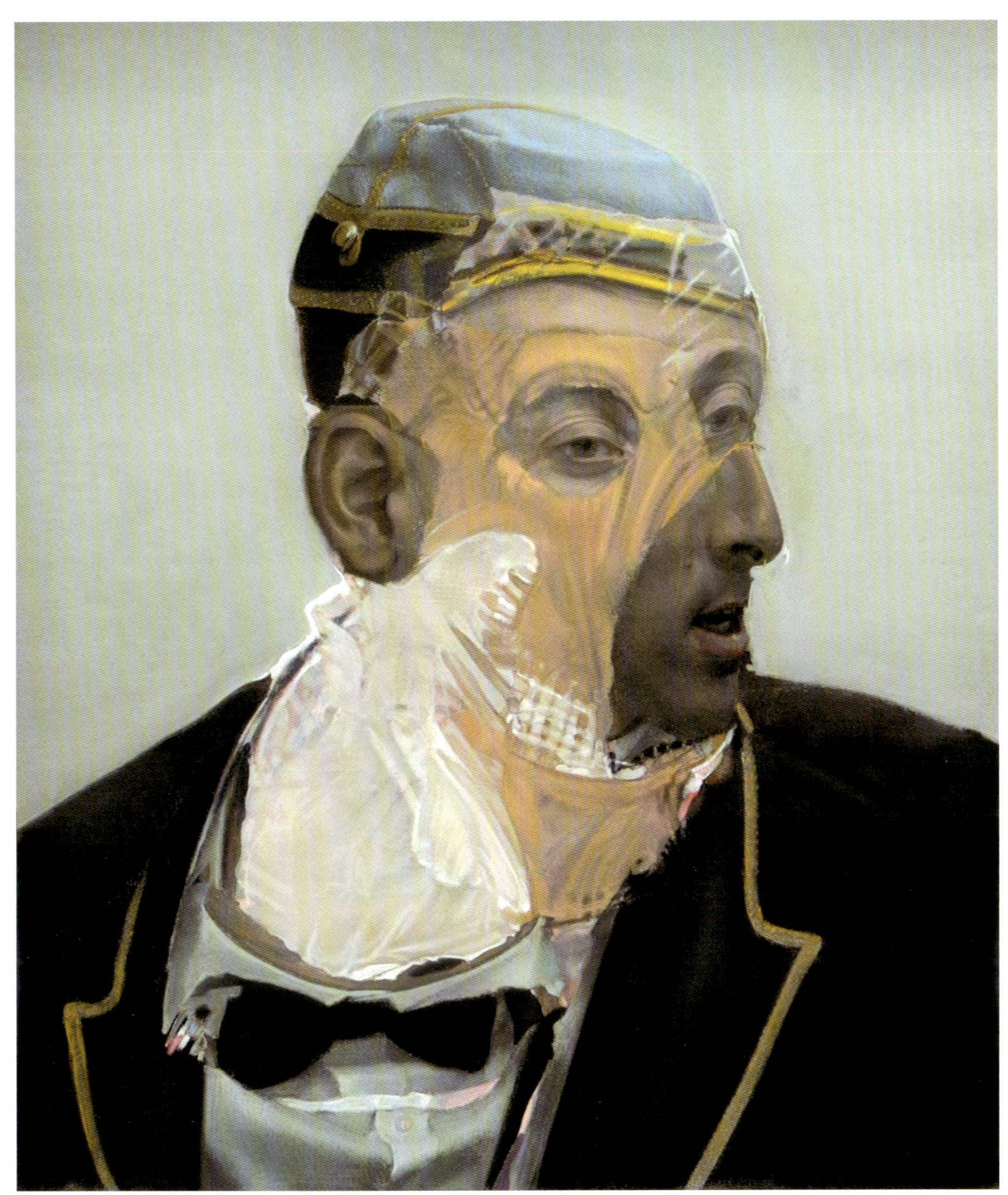

jrp|ringier

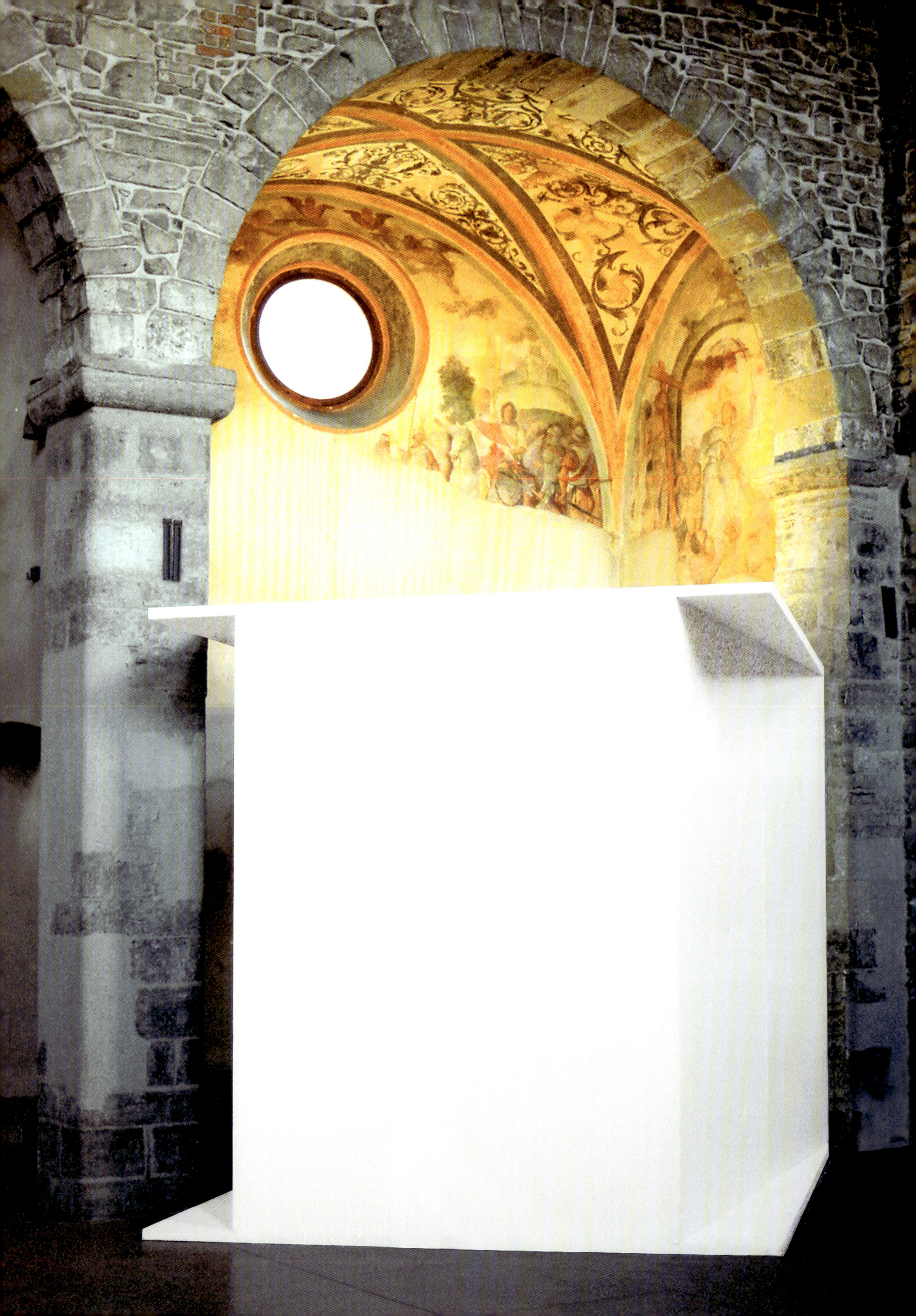

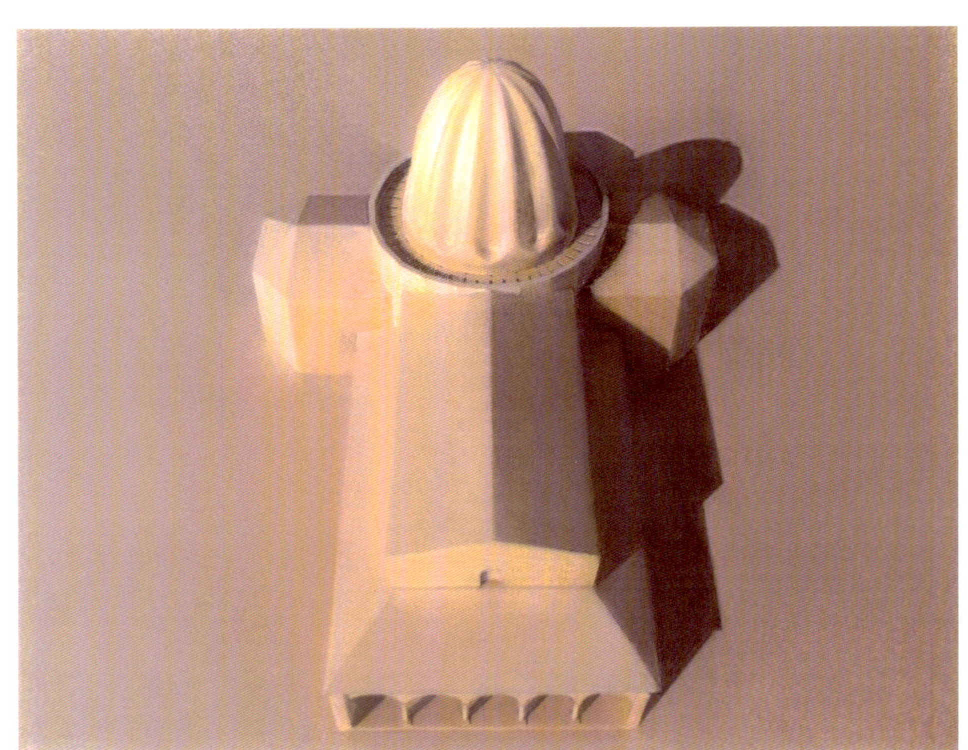

↑
UNTITLED, 2003

←
MESSAGGERIE MUSICALI, 2002

← ←
THE SKELETON KEY, 2006

← ← ←
UNTITLED, 1992

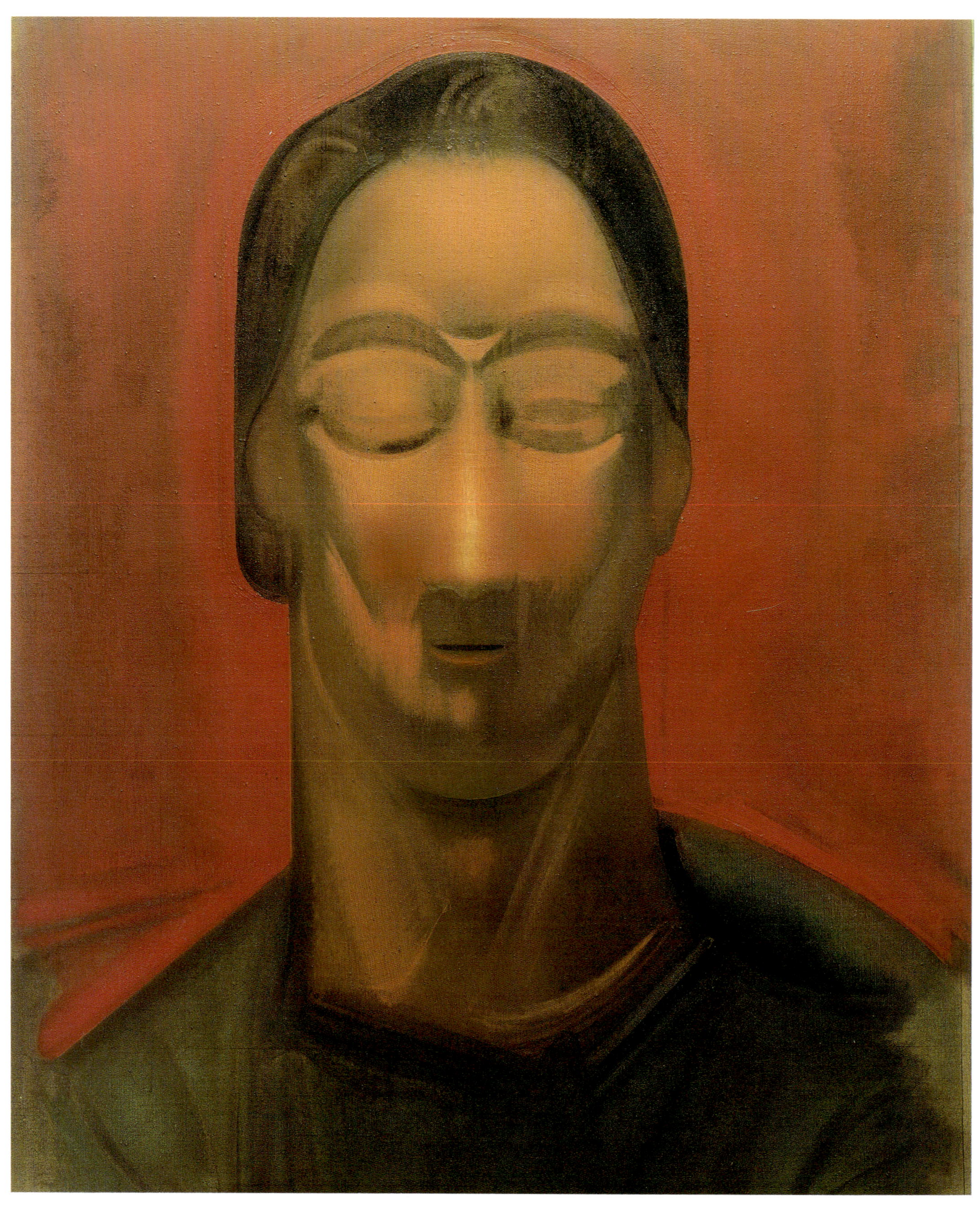

Preface to an Unwritten Essay on Pietro Roccasalva
Barry Schwabsky

I. An Ending

One might be tempted to say: This art, which is nothing but a contra-
diction of itself, does not exist.
Or if it did exist, it would be incomprehensible.
Or if it were comprehensible, it would still be incommunicable.
But that being the case, the essay should now end.
Except that I should at least give some explanation for why I say
Roccasalva's art is a contradiction of itself, shouldn't I?

II. An Antinomy

1. Roccasalva is a painter; his art can rightly be called painting.
Although his work deploys many mediums, including video, objects, and
performance, its central medium, the hub from which all his other
endeavors radiate and to which they return, is painting, and in its classical
sense: the painted picture, the *tableau*. Moreover, the investment of
skill, labor, and thought in these pictures (in oil, pastel, or tempera) is
massive, showing nothing like the nonchalance toward the medium of
those "artists who make paintings" of whom we have seen many examples.

*2. Roccasalva is not a painter, but rather a practitioner of what Thierry
de Duve has called "generic art"; his art should be called conceptual.*
Although he does produce paintings, his work ranges far beyond this
traditional medium to encompass video, objects, and performance, among
others; and while painting is a recurrent reference point for this oeuvre,
it is far from central to the work's significance. Rather, painting can be
seen here as something like what Alfred Hitchcock called a "mcguffin"—a
device that serves to set the whole artistic machine into motion but has
no intrinsic artistic significance of its own.

III. Another Antinomy

1. Roccasalva's is an open work.
Roccasalva speaks of "work situations" and "work in progress." No one
work is ever an end in itself, but rather each becomes the starting
point for another. For this reason, the work never allows either the artist
or the viewer a sense of mastery. A curving neon tube, for instance,
describes the path of a tracking shot in a video (but since the video is
animated, it is merely a virtual or imaginary tracking shot). The work
of the work is never done. It is the product and in turn the occasion of a
desire that is endless—that is to say, of an obsession, or in any case
of a project that is always straining beyond its own contingent boundaries.

2. Roccasalva's work is hermetic, closed in on itself.
An image of a partly eaten bread roll takes on the aspect of a human
skull—the stuff of life becomes a memento mori, but in a derisive sense;
by the same token, a lemon squeezer becomes the model for the dome of
a cathedral—or is it vice versa? In this endless train of associations
(where, moreover, the exalted and the trivial become fatally confused)
everything always refers to something else somewhere in the artist's
oeuvre. Connect the dots, and the lines of connection will weave a circle
around a void. Black paint on a neon light cancels out the appearance
of light, but not its existence.

IV. A Precursor

Marcel Duchamp said that the viewer completes the work. And indeed a
bad work of art is precisely the one with no need of a viewer to complete
it. I have always believed that an artwork should leave an empty space
for me. And just for me. Roland Barthes put it this way: "The book you
write must prove to me *that it desires me*." Or consider what the doorkeeper
says to the man from the country in Kafka's *Before the Law*: "This door
was intended only for you."

However, Pietro Roccasalva has done something else: made a work in
which I've disappeared. As I walked through his exhibition in Turin last
year, *My Private #4*, it was if I was wandering through a dream which
was taking place in order to be perceived by me but at which I was not
present, gazing into a mirror in which my reflection does not appear.
Each thing I saw had a strange power of fascination in itself yet always
directed me to an "elsewhere." Duchamp's peephole—the one in *Étant
donnés*—fixes me in an embarrassed self-consciousness. Roccasalva's,
in *Jockey Full of Bourbon*, absents me: my non-appearance completes
the work.

V. A Doubt

Perhaps I'm not absent to this work after all. I might be just around the
corner—running late. Roccasalva has said the same of himself: "The
artificer as conscious individual always arrives late." The owl we see in
Jockey Full of Bourbon would then be the very one mentioned long ago
by G.W.F. Hegel, the one that takes wing at dusk: wisdom herself. But
tarted up as a parrot? Perhaps this is the owl of folly—of imitation rather
than insight. On which side does art find itself? Both at once, it seems.
Another antinomy: art as illusion, art as truth. Or rather, art as the
truth about illusions, or as an illusion that tells the truth. Mystification
and demystification, lunacy and lucidity, illness and cure. A serious game.
Roccasalva has explicitly identified himself with the sophist Gorgias,
quoting the words (in Giorgio Colli's Italian translation): "chi inganna è
più giusto di chi non inganna e chi è ingannatio è piú sapiente di chi
non è ingannato"—"a deceiver is more just than one who does not deceive,
and the deceived is wiser than the undeceived." More recently, Slavoj
Zizek has said the same thing in his own way by punning on Jacques Lacan's

famous phrase "le nom du père"; for Zizek, "les non-dupes errent"—
those who are not fooled, the undeceived, err.

When I enter into the ever-shifting, never-entirely unequivocal world of
Pietro Roccasalva, am I allowing myself the pleasure of being deceived or
do I demand of myself the effort to cast off illusions? Can someone tell me?

VI. A Beginning

No, don't tell me. It would be better to say: This art, which is entirely
a contradiction of itself, does not exist.
Or if it did exist, it would be incomprehensible.
Or if it were comprehensible, it would still be incommunicable.
That being the case, the essay should now end.
Only, since the truth is unbelievable, even the person who by chance comes
to speak it cannot act in consistency with it.
Therefore, the essay can now begin.

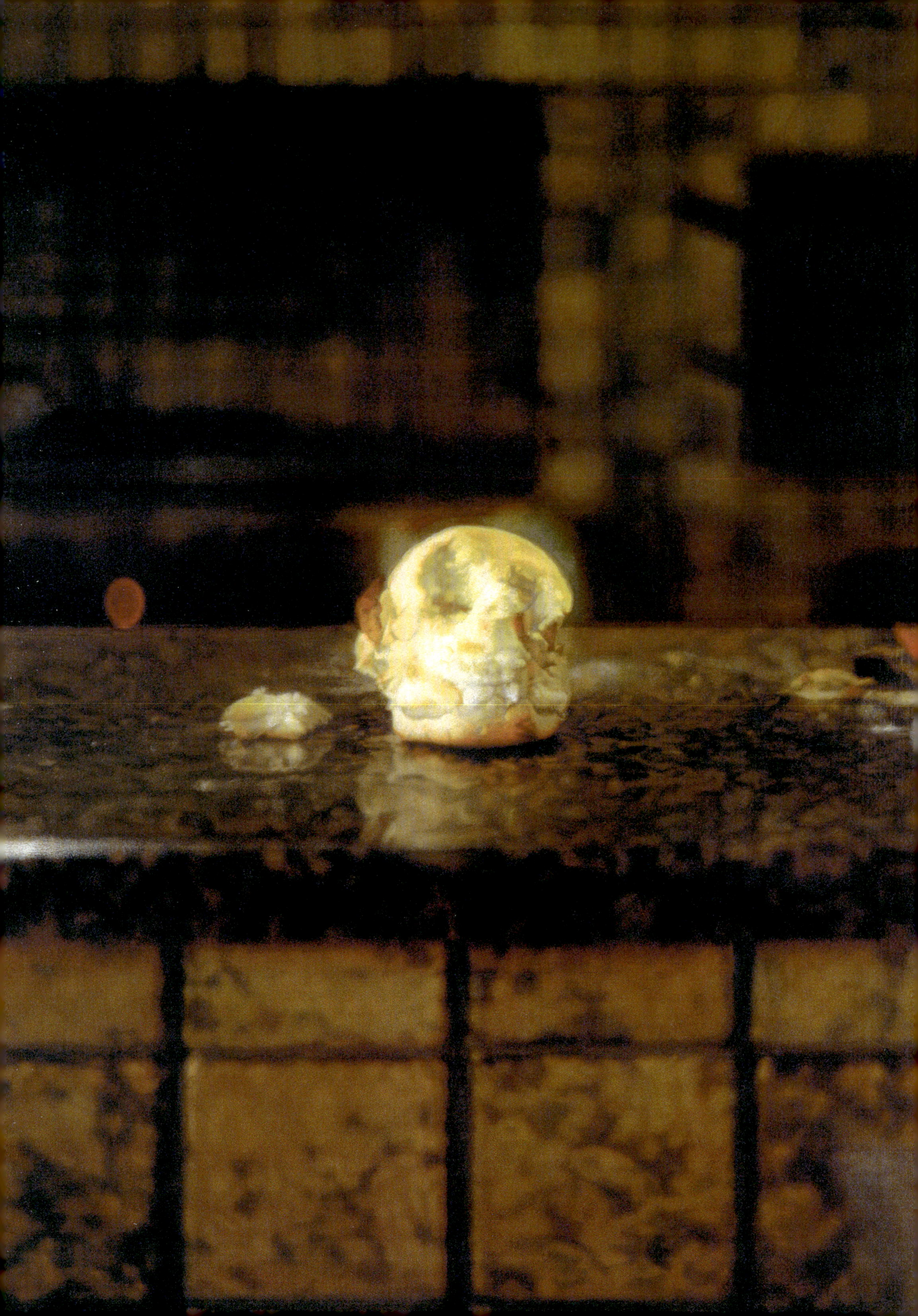

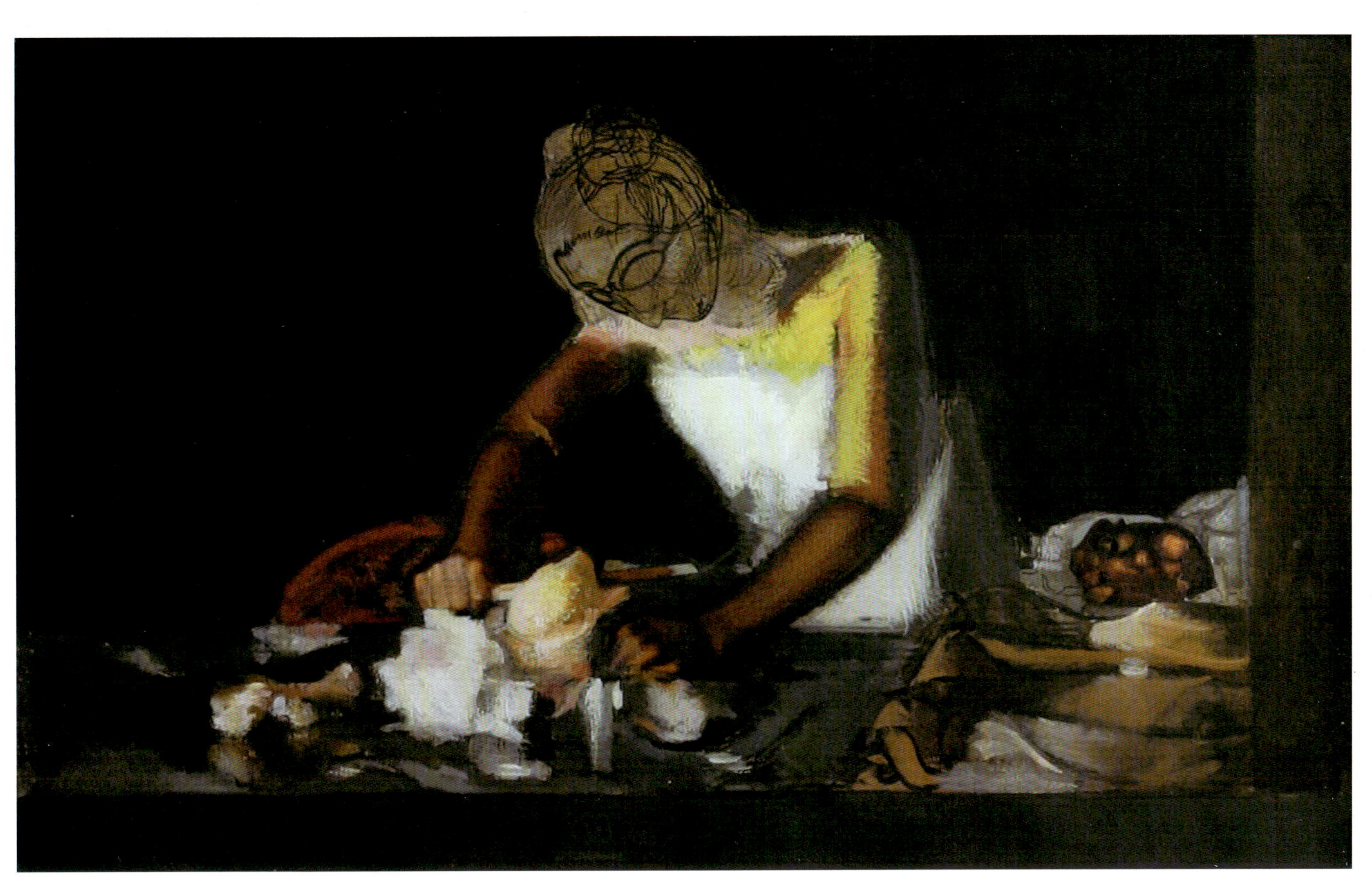

↑
UNTITLED, 2006

←
UNTITLED, 2003 (detail)

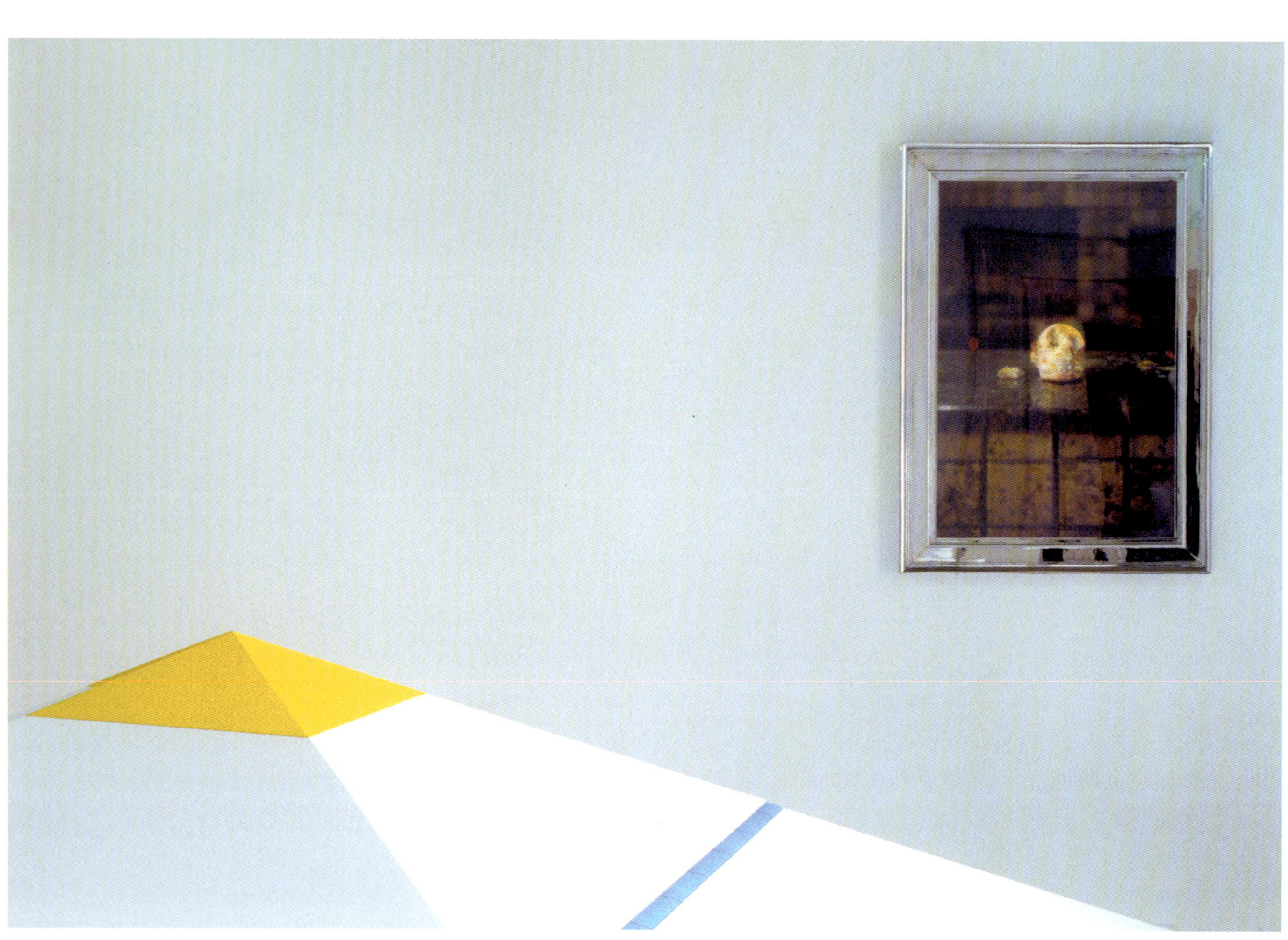

FISHEYE, 2003

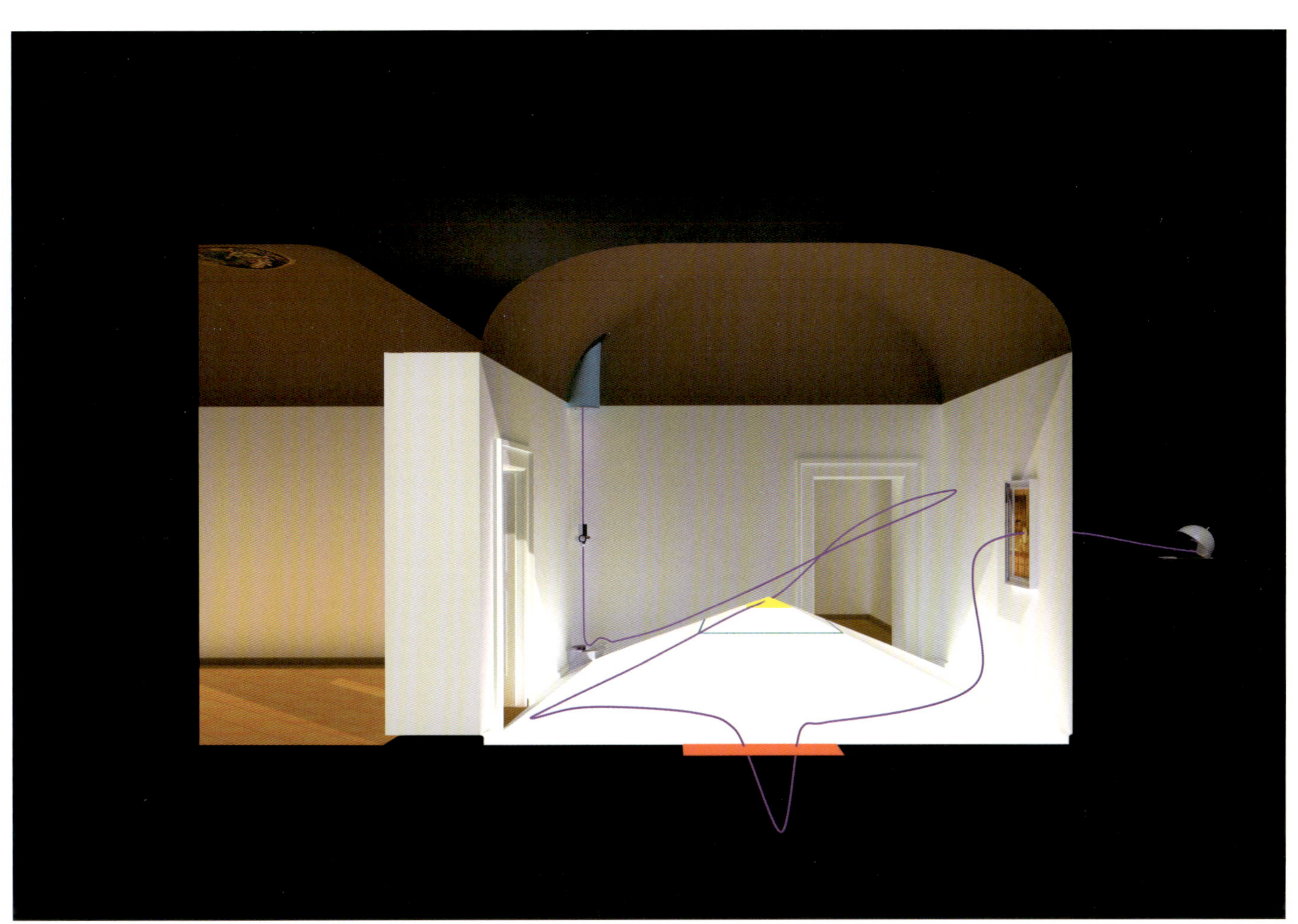

FISHEYE, 2003

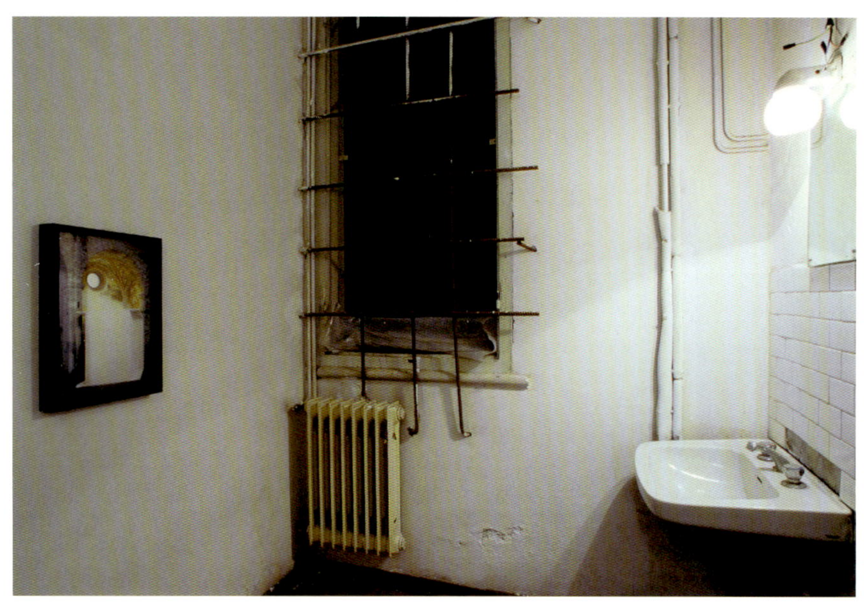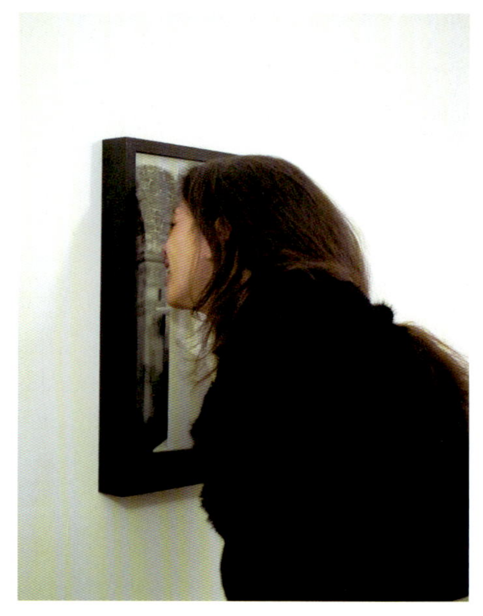

↑
JOCKEY FULL OF BOURBON, 2003

→
JOCKEY FULL OF BOURBON, 2005

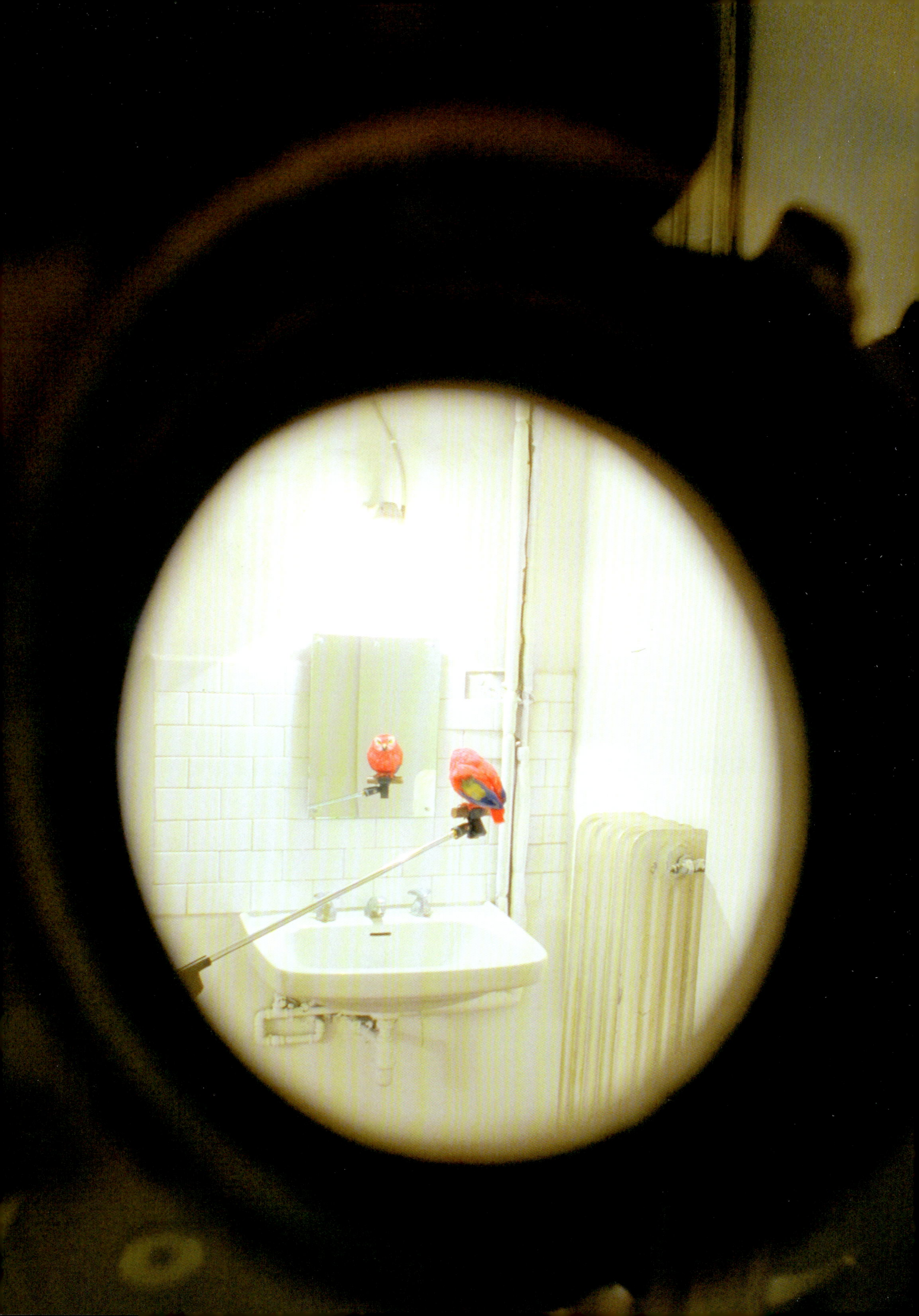

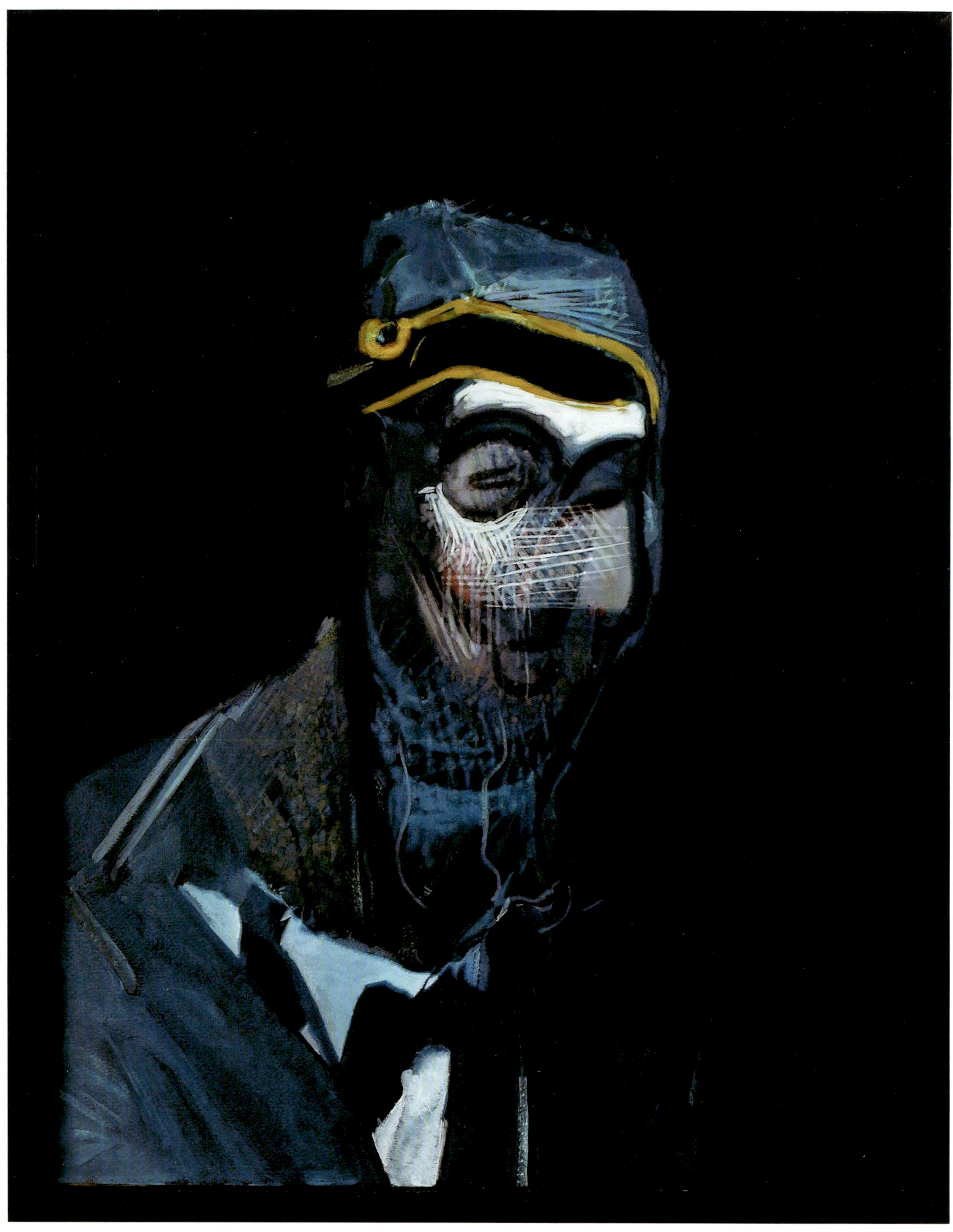

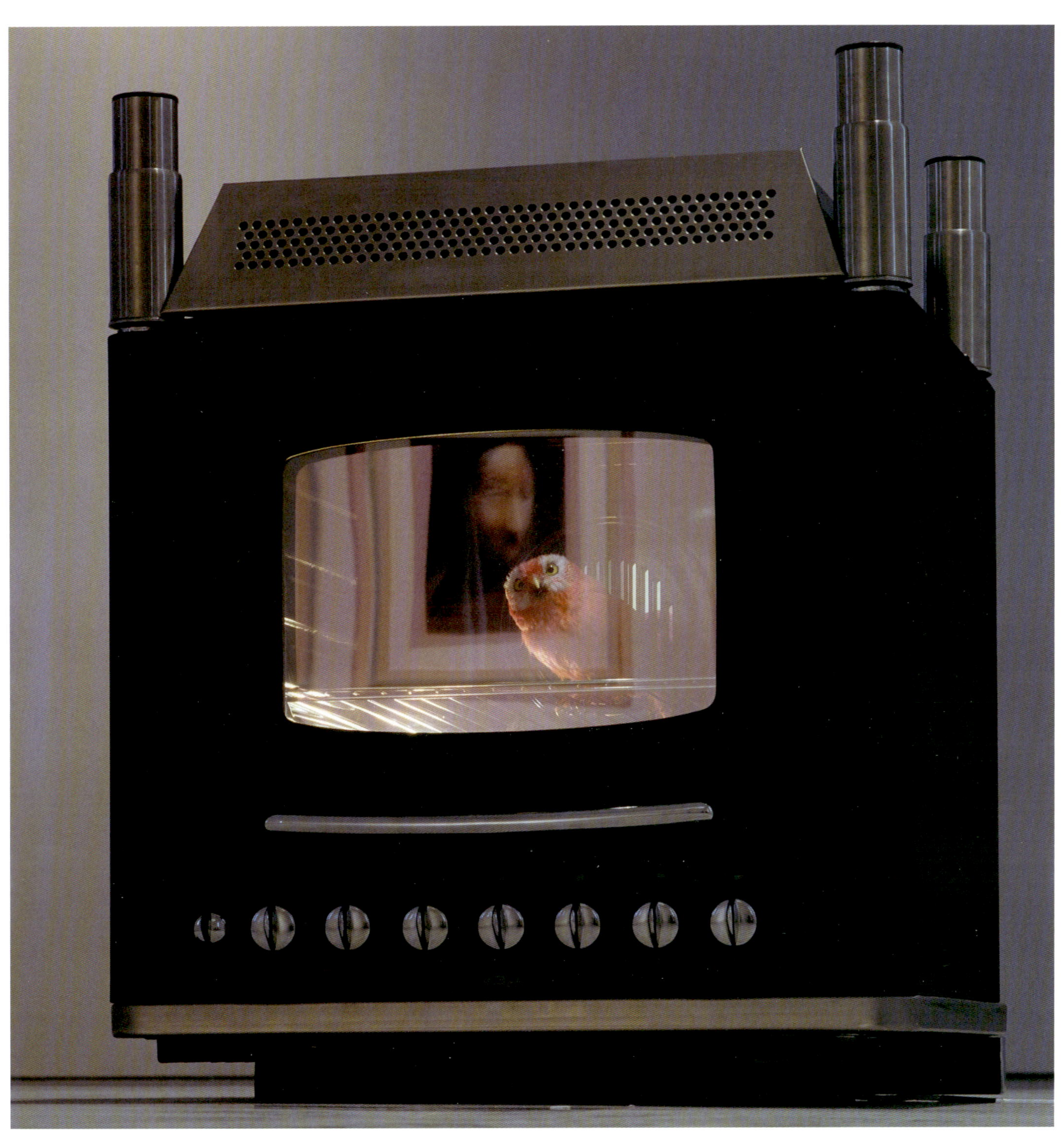

REX, 2004

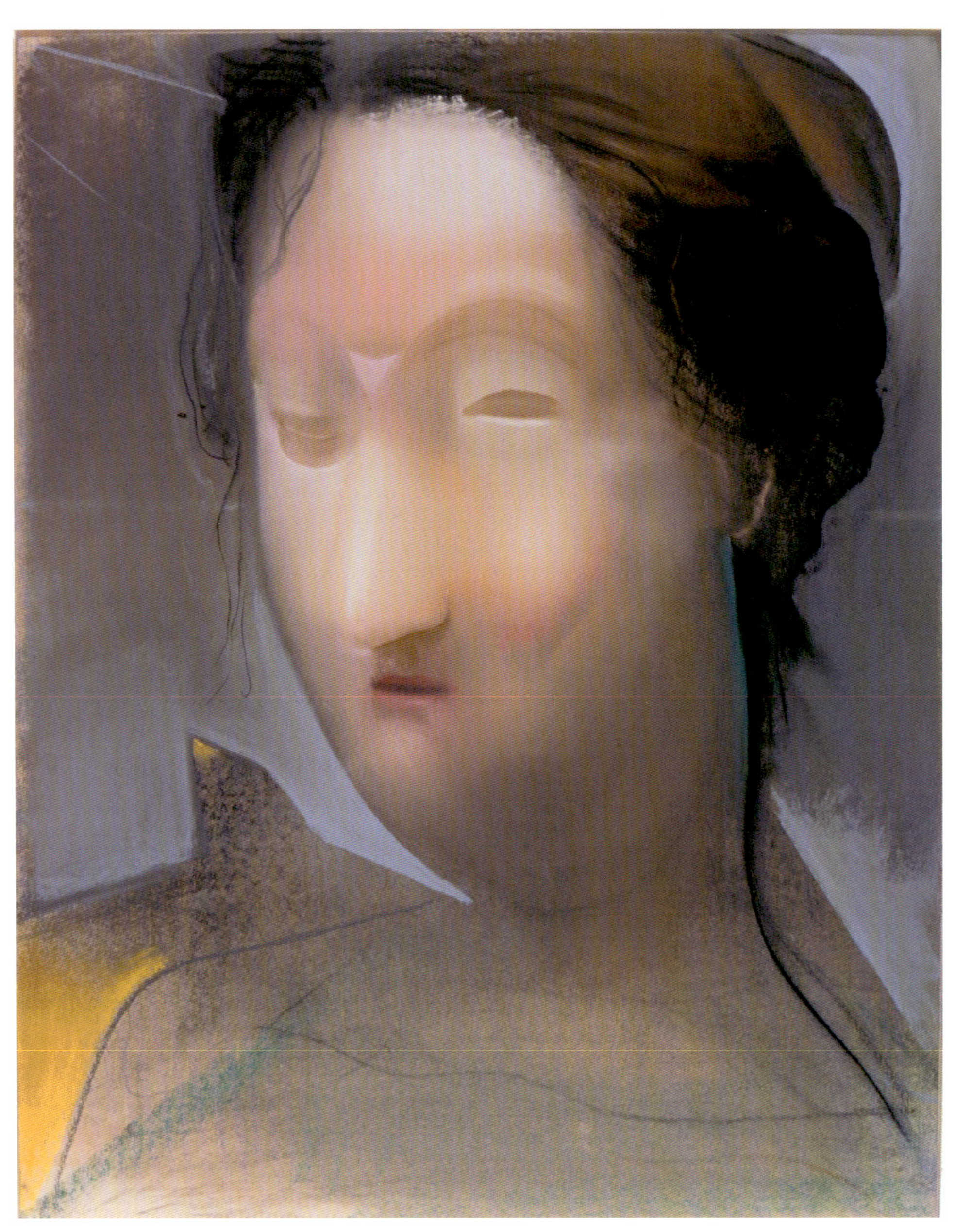

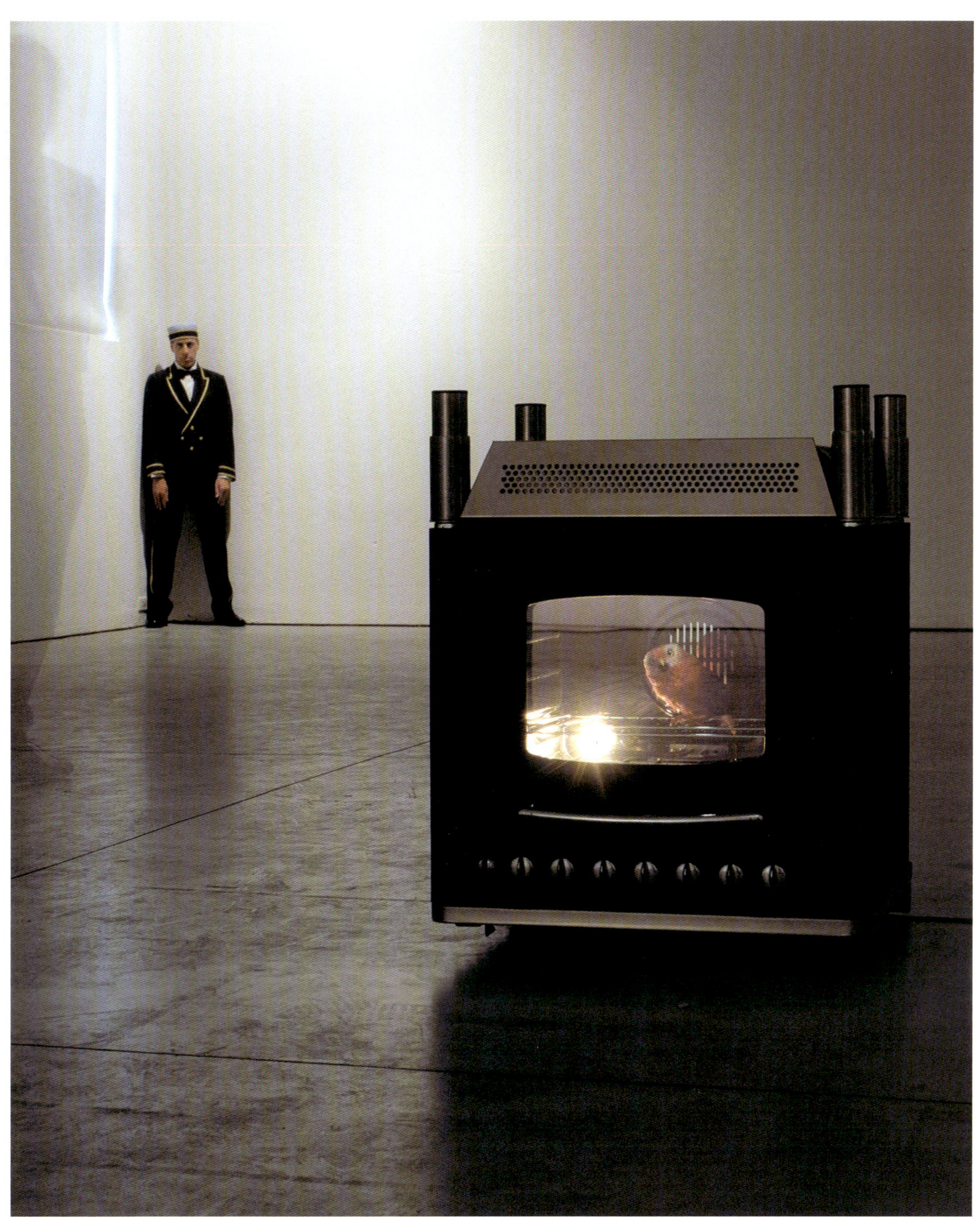

O.H. SITUAZIONE D'OPERA IN QUATTRO STANZE, 2004

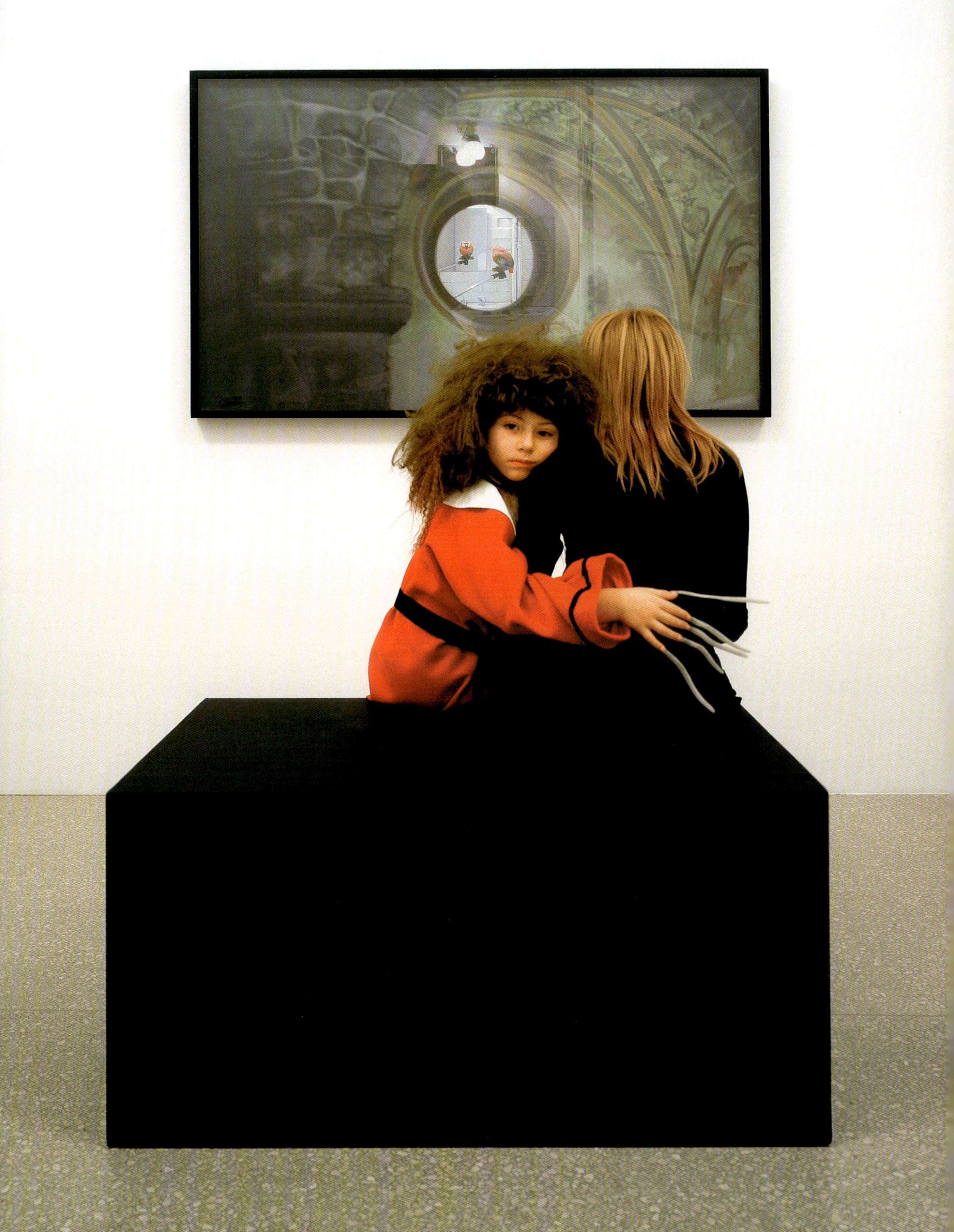

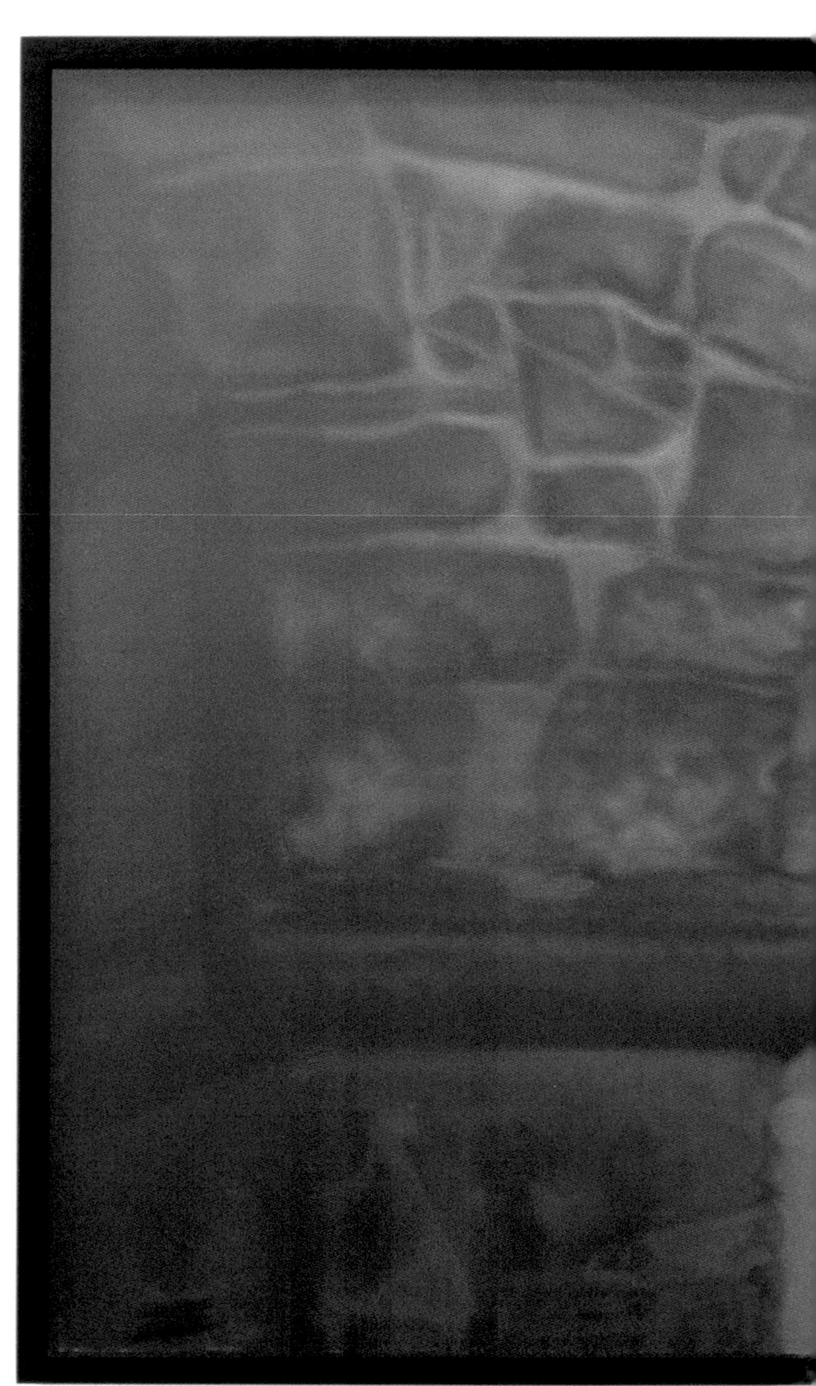

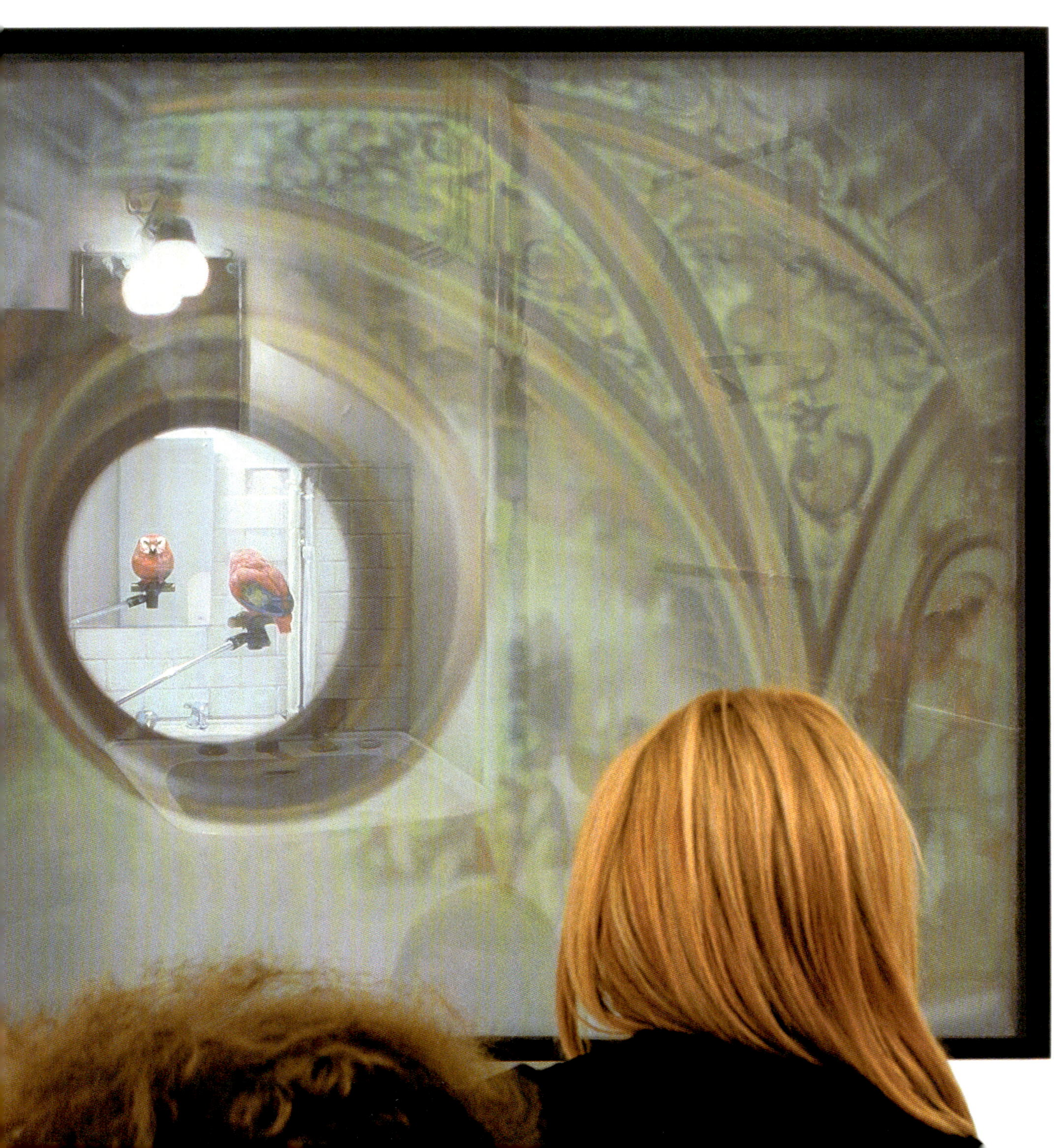

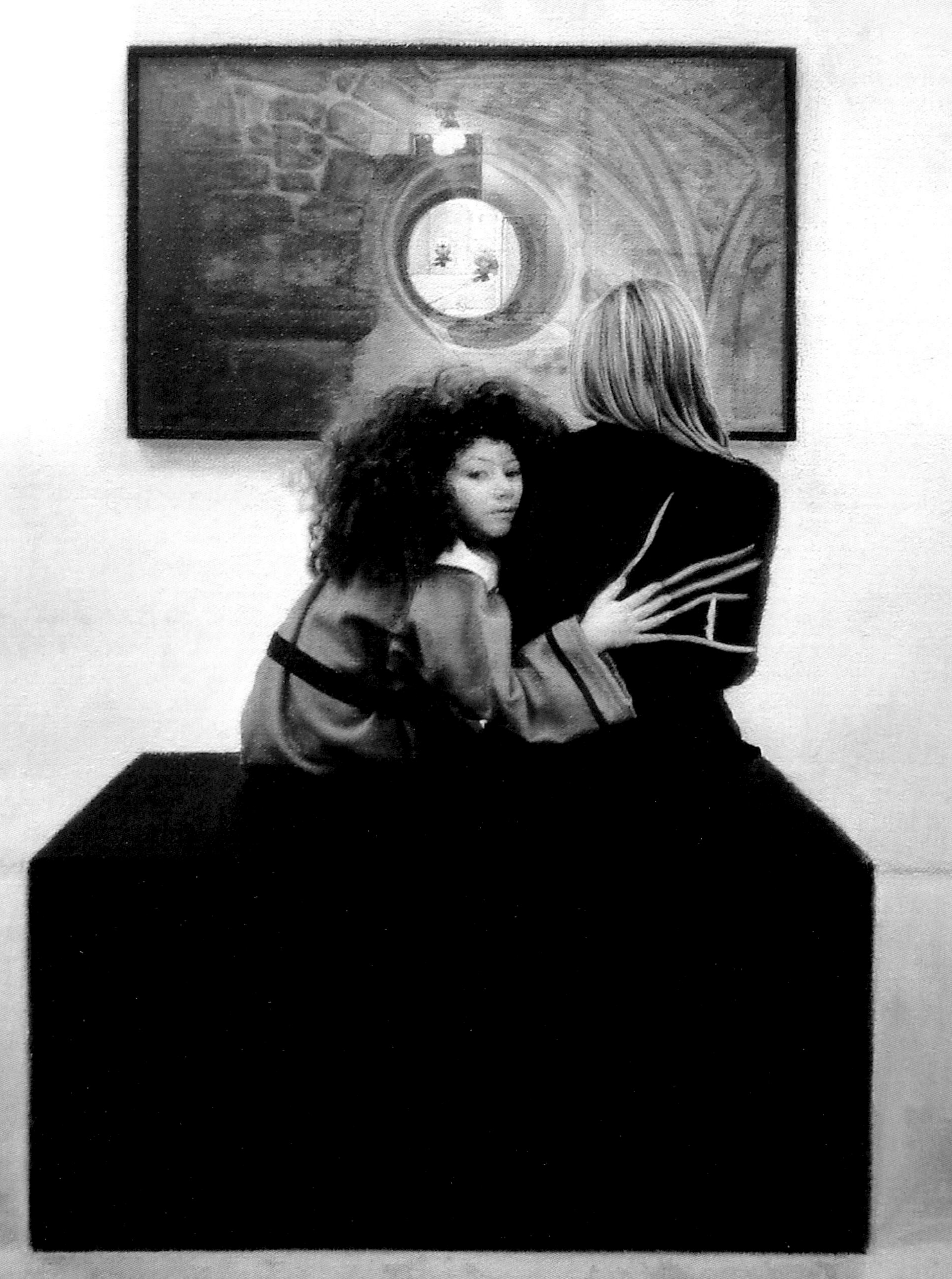

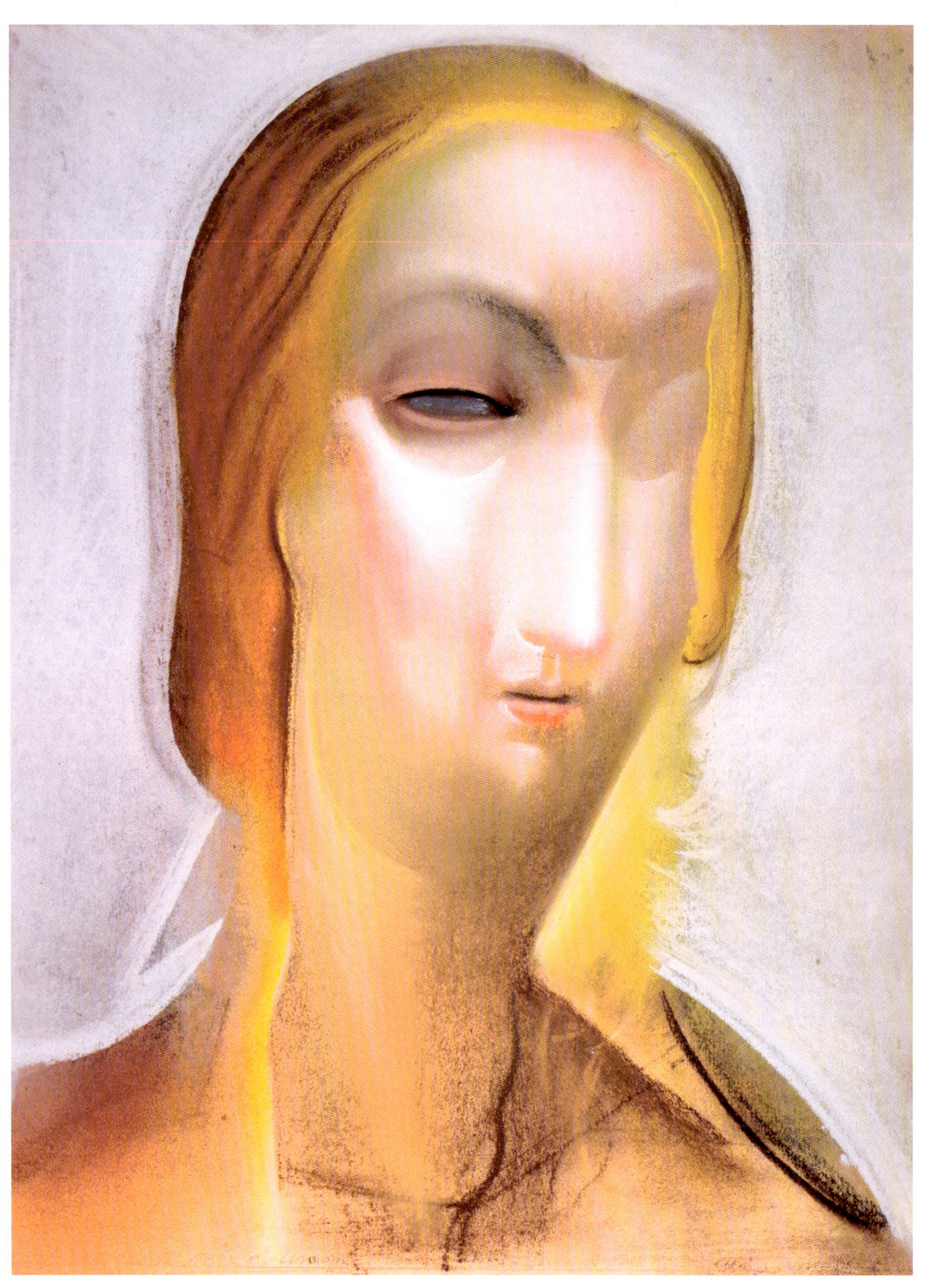

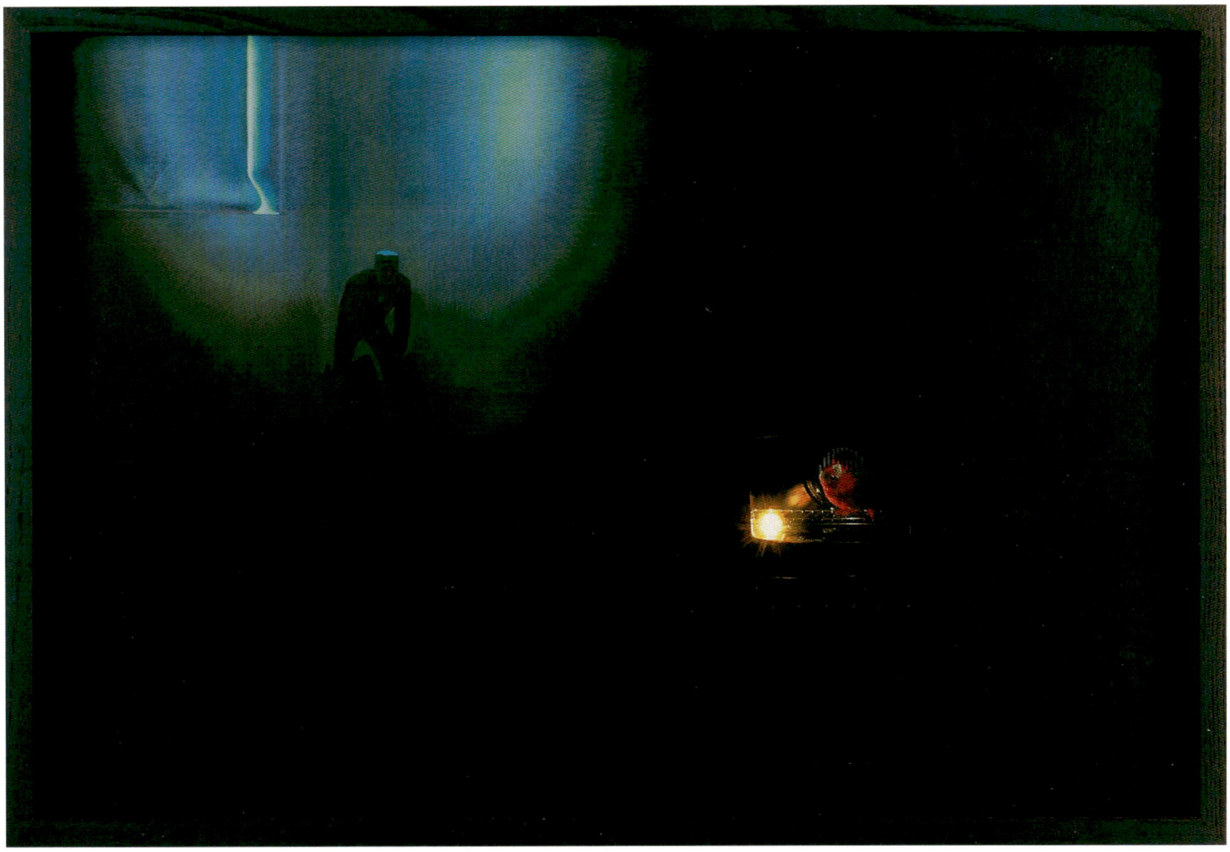

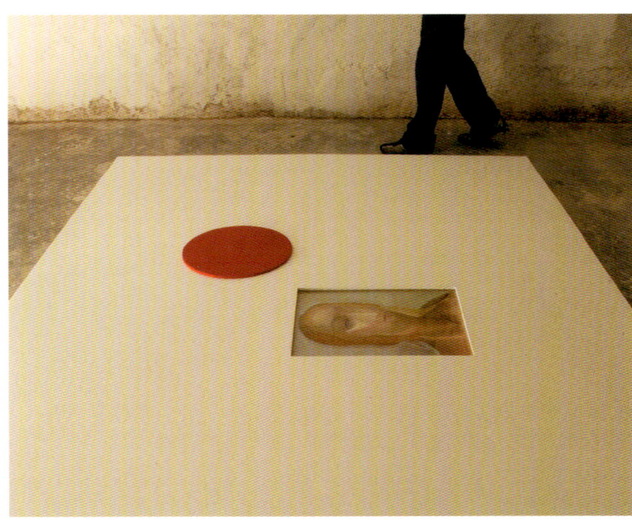

↑
UNTITLED, 2005

← / ← ←
THE GOOD WOMAN, 2005

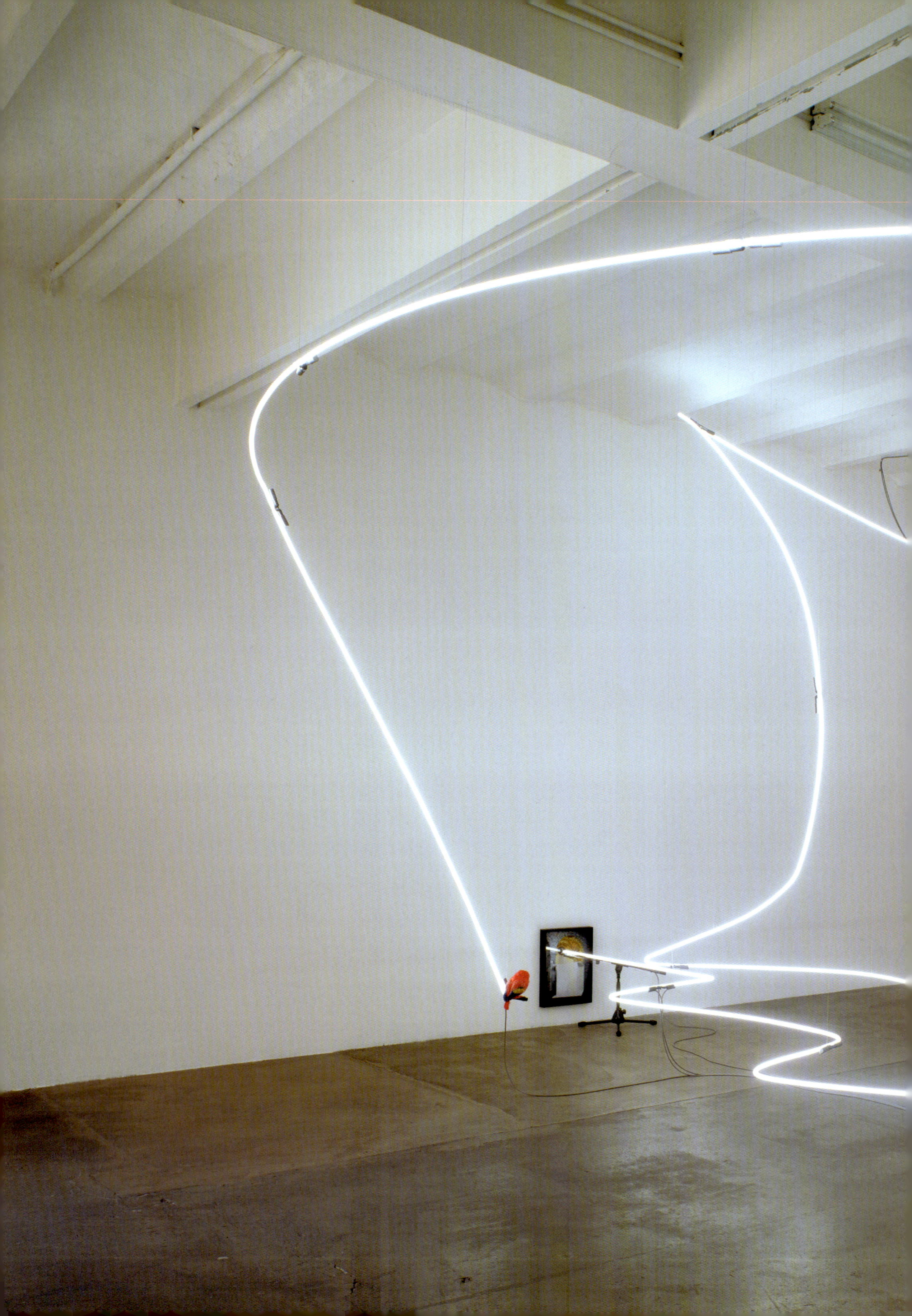

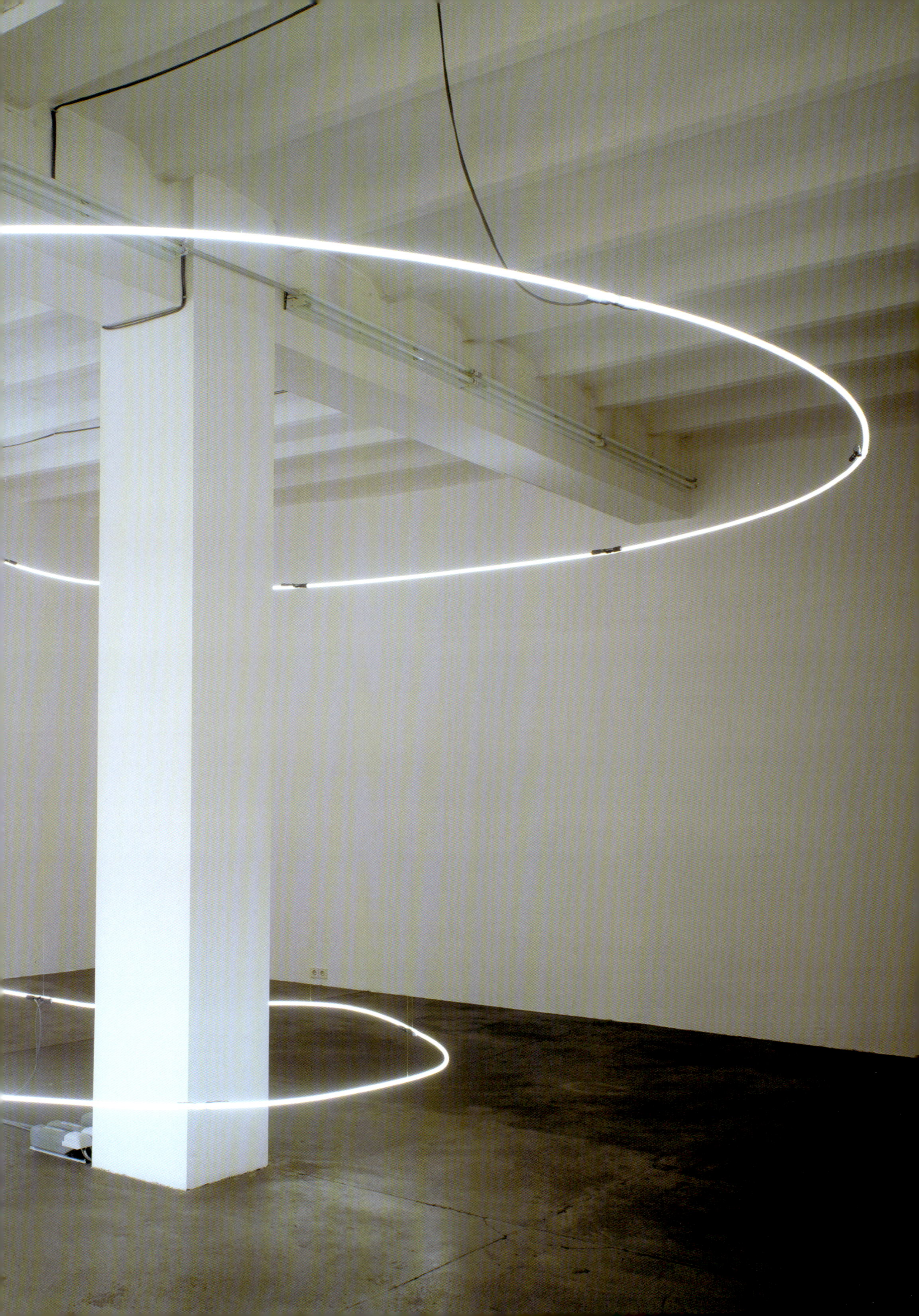

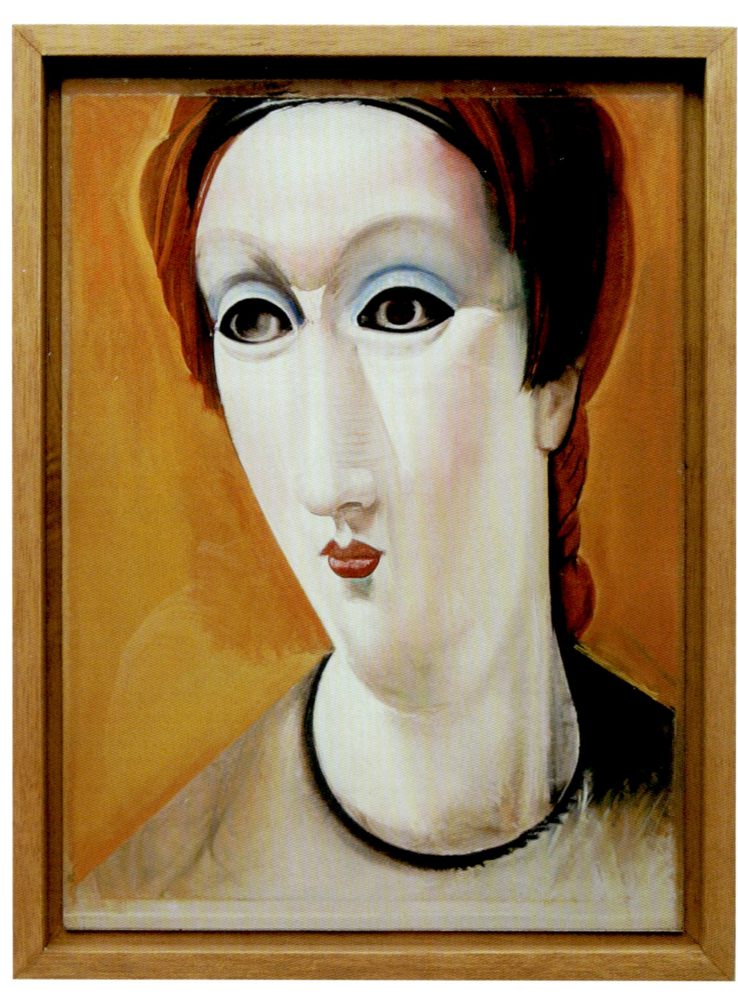

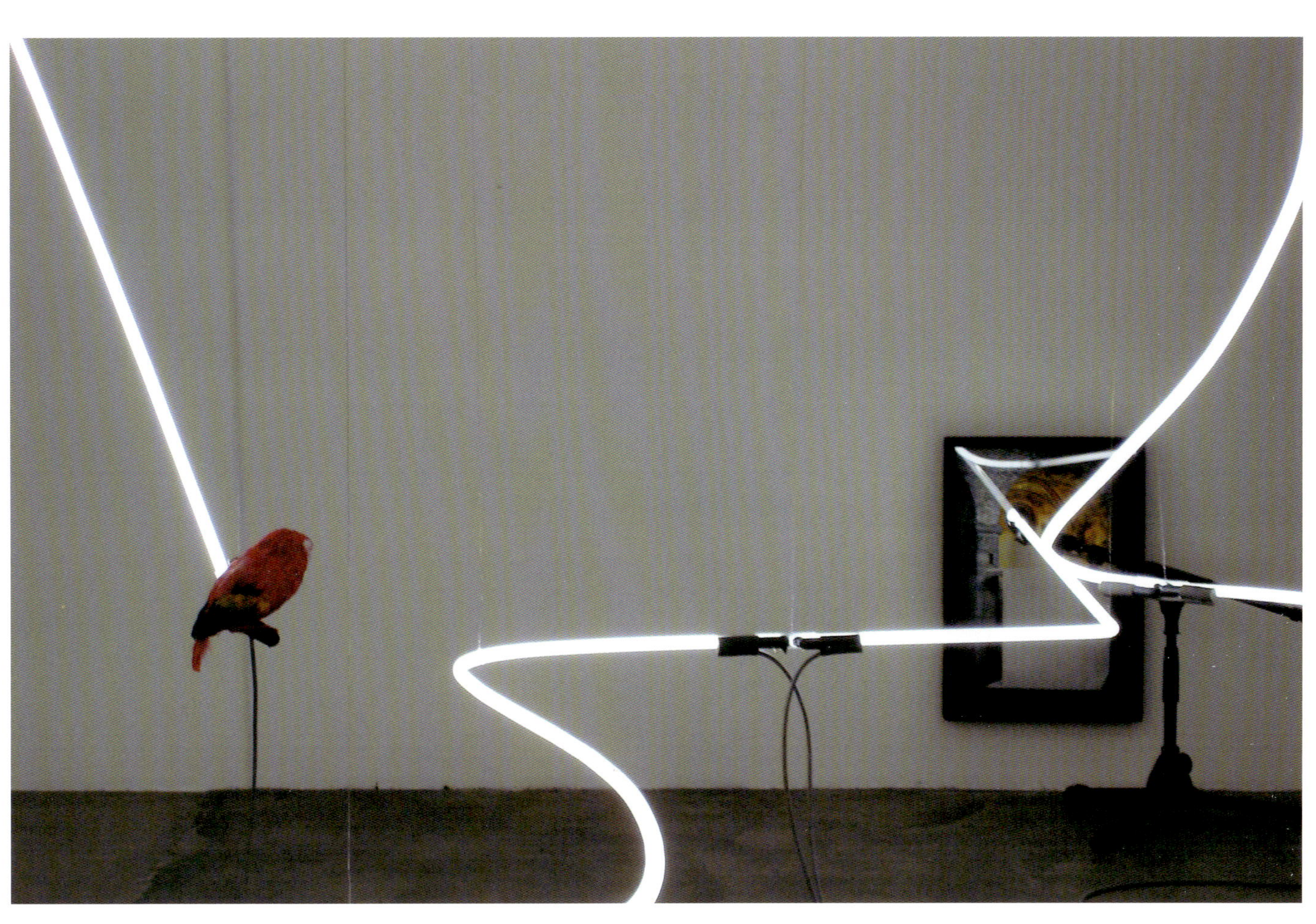

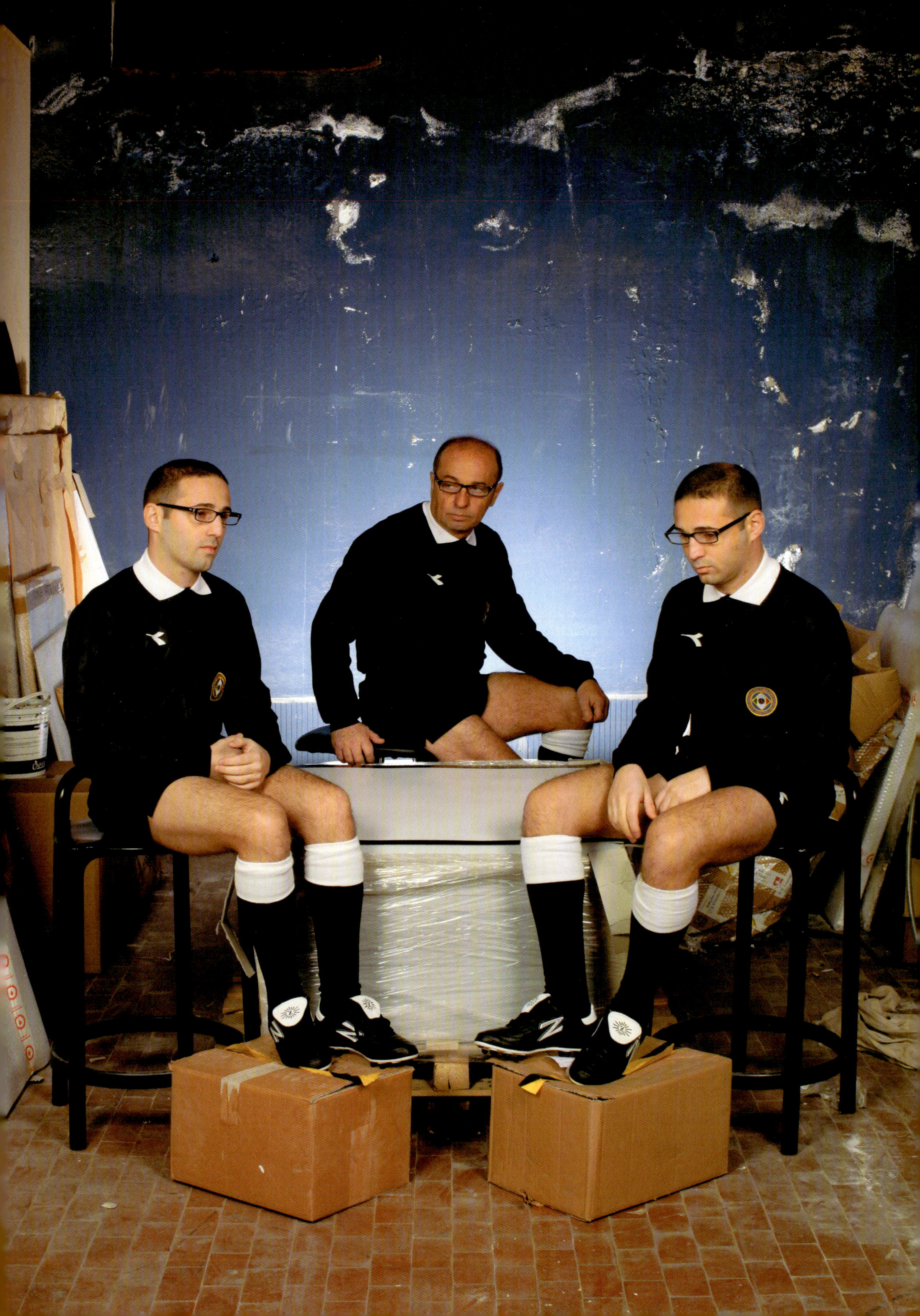

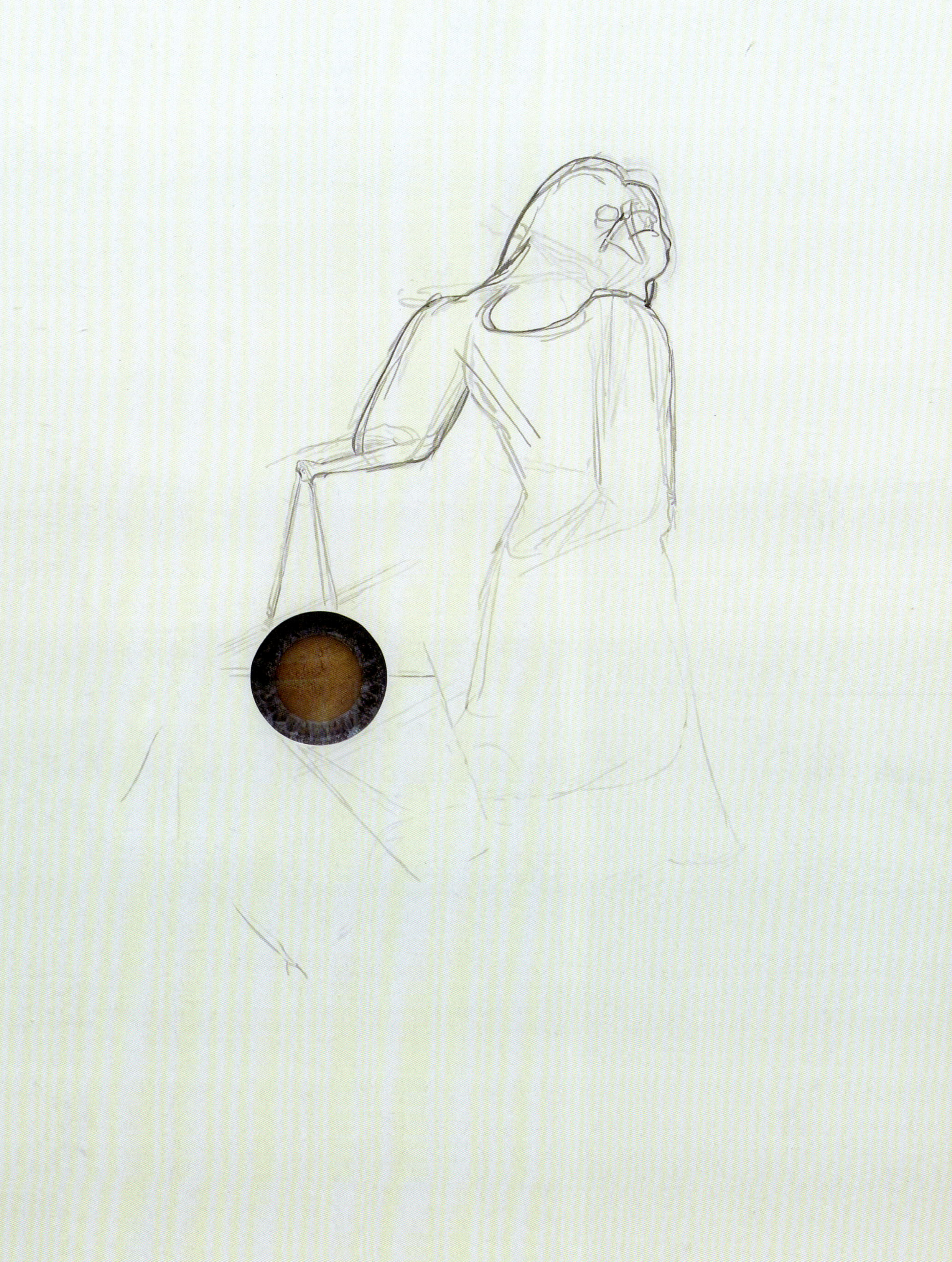

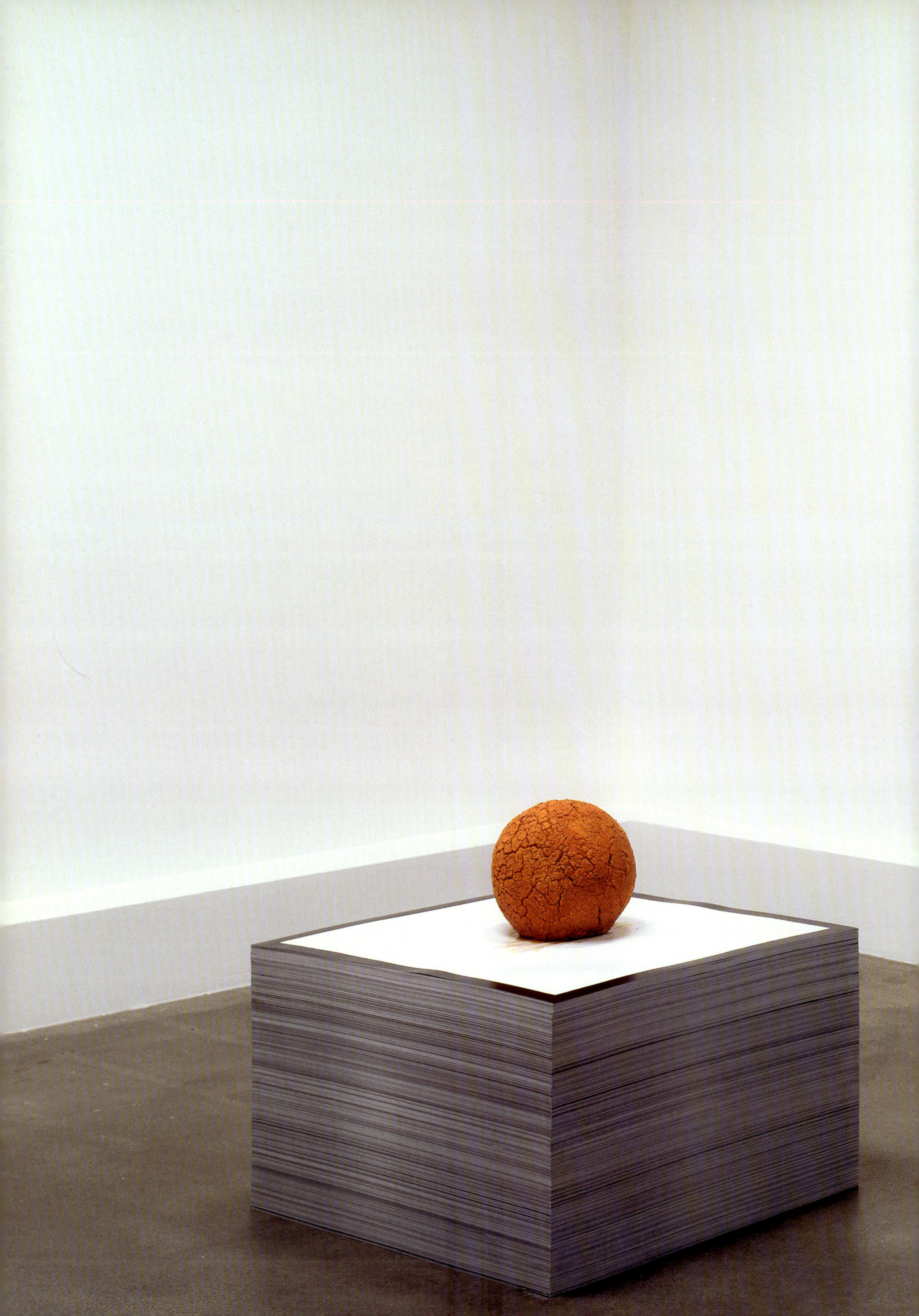

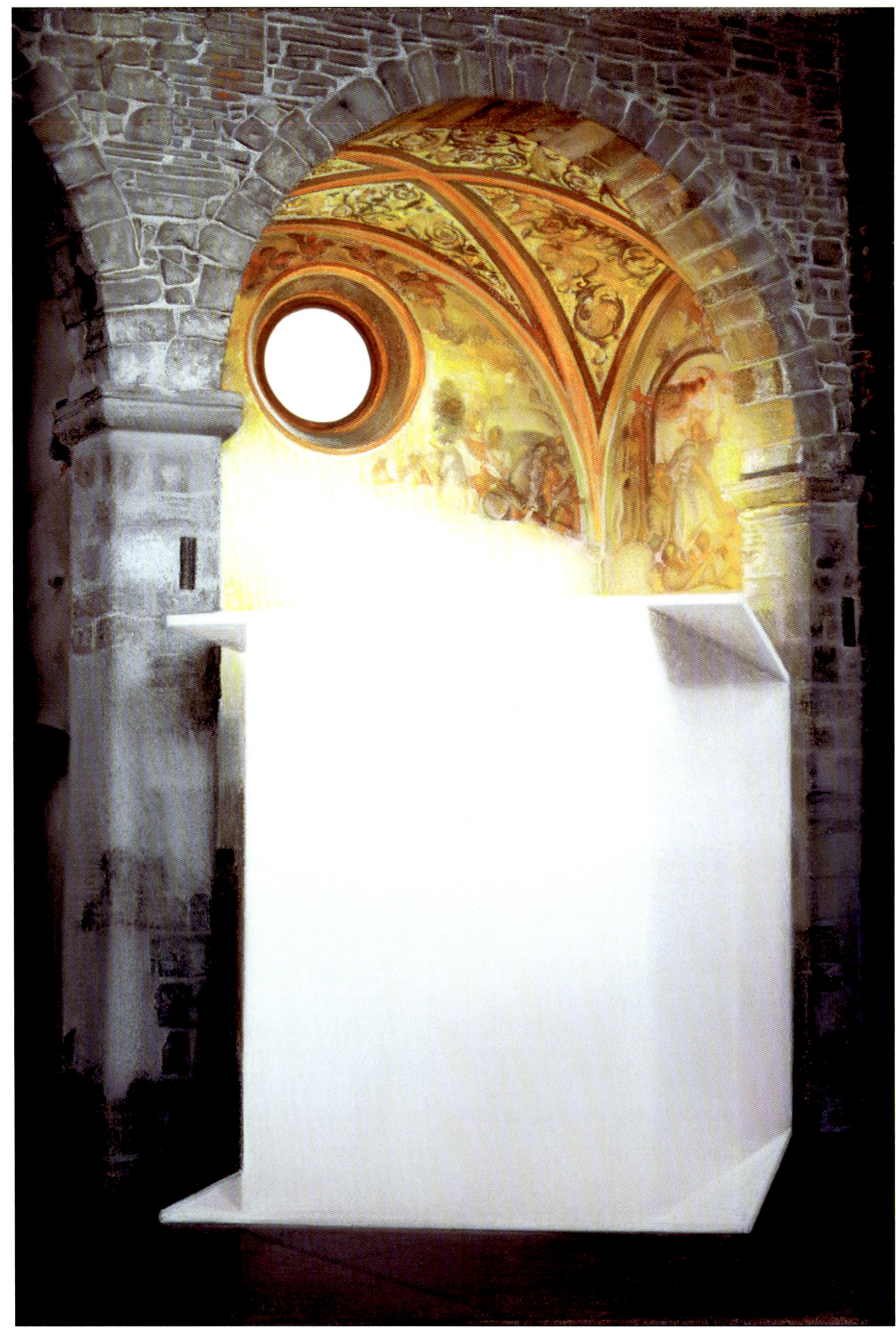

←
UNTITLED, 2003

← ←
D'APRÈS LA TEMPESTA, 2006

← ← ←
THE SILENT WOMAN, 2007

← ← ← ←
STUDY FOR Z, 2007

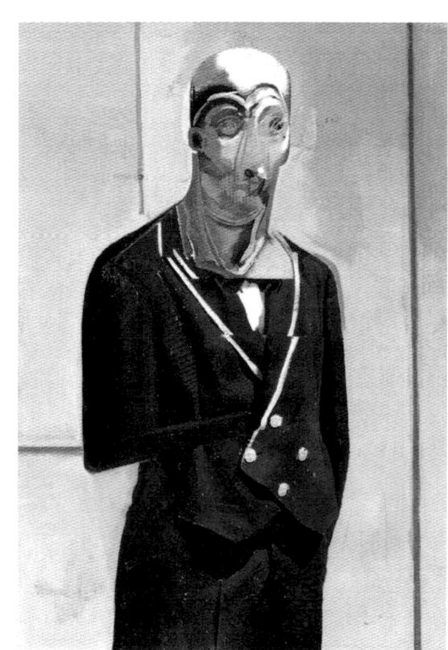

STUDY FOR THE SKELETON KEY, 2007

Pietro Roccasalva is an eccentric artist with a singular visual universe. In the recent years of visionariness, nightmare, and inner obsession, Roccasalva's eccentricity, rather than exhausts itself in a repertory of incongruous objects and presences, expresses itself in a deeper valency attributed to the image as a depository for many textual references. This is why his work may be accused of hermetism, if by hermetism we mean the production of a symbolic universe that feeds on citations from ancient painting, mystic thought, or philosophy, in which this universe is faced with a widespread belief that the function of art is global communication. And one must admit that many of the images produced by Roccasalva, while they may be bereft of the magical power of the symbol, at least imply and preserve the symbol's intellective structure.

That his is a "closed" universe is a fact that the artist himself affirms in an explicit manner, when he incorporates the images of his worksite and workshop to describe the process that lies at the foundations of his work. Cathedrals, particularly Gothic ones, are stratifications of interventions that have accumulated over time: the succession of many generations of designers and artists over the centuries results in the articulation of the attributes of time—meaning the passing and becoming —within the architectural and visual space. In this way, for Roccasalva, every single work is part of a process, the element of a concatenation of mobile objects, in which a painting may become the gravitational center of a tableau vivant that, in turn, will become a starting point for a pictorial or object representation, along a timeline where the latter is reproduced through digital simulation or in an installation. It is no accident if Roccasalva chooses to use the image of a gothic worksite as a metaphor for the procedure through which his work absorbs heterogeneity and attempts to structure it within an organic identity. It is not accidental precisely because the space of Gothic architecture is not just a theater for drawings, plans, and visions that are not realized by their own creators and that, because of this, unfurl over time, but also because in this succession of posthumous and delayed executions it becomes the historic and specific backdrop for a progressive emersion, that of the idea of an artist as an individualized person, who differentiates himself and stands out with respect to the workshop environment. And yet the long Gothic era remains a kind of passage; it does not represent the finished stage of this process of individualization of the artist and, because of this, it preserves a dialectic matrix between conception and execution, anonymity and singularity, will and determination of the results. It is an era of becoming in which forms are fixed and an eccentric imagination begins with the idea of "monstrum" (meaning something extraneous and irreducible), and which looks toward the conquest of eternity and the inorganic.

In order to define the components that from time to time structure his personal worksite, Roccasalva uses the expression "situazione d'opera" (work situations), a group of "objects, furnishings, audiovisuals, actions, tableaux vivants, etc. that cohabit with other paintings and decline all the phases of painterly creation."[1] And what is striking is the implicit *temporality* inherent to the idea of "situation." It is as if it belonged to something that had its own duration—a mobility in time—that is transitory, just like the ephemeral Baroque apparatuses that, paradoxically, are the opposite of the Gothic cathedral in their function as structures, which, while on the one hand are responsible for the celebration of an eternal divinity, on the other, carry out this function within the performativity limited within the time of their own earthly condition. In narrating his own work almost as if it were a saga, the artist mentions Zurvan, the pre-Islamic Persian god of time. Also in reference to this the artist says: "The entirety of the 'situazione d'opera' [may] gradually develop as a single story in [episodes] or a poem in 'whims,' of which, however, Zurvan is the author. Unlike the Greek Kronos … Zurvan Akarana is time as a 'situation' in which his twin sons Ohrmazd and Ahriman, respectively the divine principals of lightness and darkness, contend over the dominion of creation with thermal battles that last for entire cycles."[2]

In a certain way, all of Pietro Roccasalva's work revolves around these figures: the images that *will materialize*, their secret nature of textual architectures, the becoming of forms, art and language as attempts to empty life of its own founding contradiction, or the organic nature, the obsolescence, and the entropy.

Starting with the photographic documentation of an installation, Roccasalva produces a painting that, in a second moment, becomes the center of another installation, the photographic recording of which becomes the basis of another painting. Looking at his work as a process is the equivalent of encountering the same image under different guises, as happens in the case of *The Oval Portrait. A Ventriloquist at a Birthday Party in October 1947* (p. 21), a tableau vivant from 2005 in which a kind of hybrid maternity (a mother dressed in contemporary clothes and her child in costume) contemplates a pastel with the same title in the presence of the public (p. 22-23). The work in question is the transposition of a photograph that documents the particulars of an installation from 2003 entitled *Jockey Full of Bourbon* (p. 14), in which a small pastel with a hole in it allowed viewers to peek into an adjacent room and consider it in relation to the room they were in, and thereby spy on the sculpture of an owl made up as a parrot that stared back at them from his roost on the pole of a microphone, reflected in a mirror. Beneath the pastel (p. 36), which acted as a diaphragm and spy hole, was the photographic rendering of *Messaggerie Musicali* (p. 4), the installation that Roccasalva realized in the decommissioned church of San Francesco in Como a year earlier. What in the photograph of the installation is a round opening in the wall of a niche in the church, became the opening in the pastel through which visitors could see into the other half of the work, and which acted as a vector for *Jockey Full of Bourbon*. In the same way, *The Oval Portrait* faithfully reproduces all that the camera recorded; thus, not only the designated surface, but also the reflection of the room on the glass of the frame as it was captured by the camera.

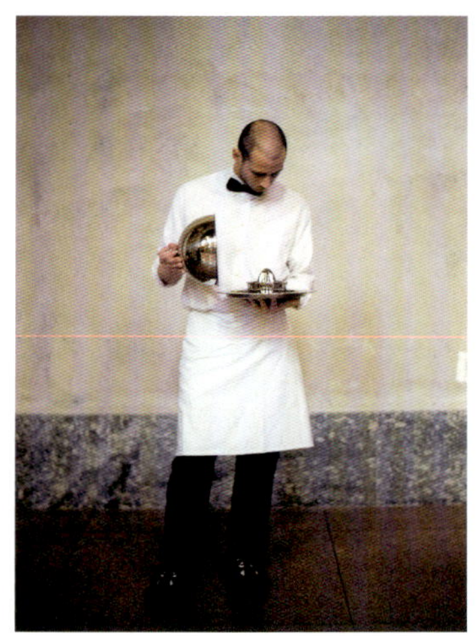

UNTITLED, 2002

1
Unpublished note from the artist.

2
Conversation between the artist and Barbara Casavecchia, "Pietro Roccasalva. Opera e fuori-opera," *Flash Art*, no. 261, December 2006–January 2007, p. 98–101.

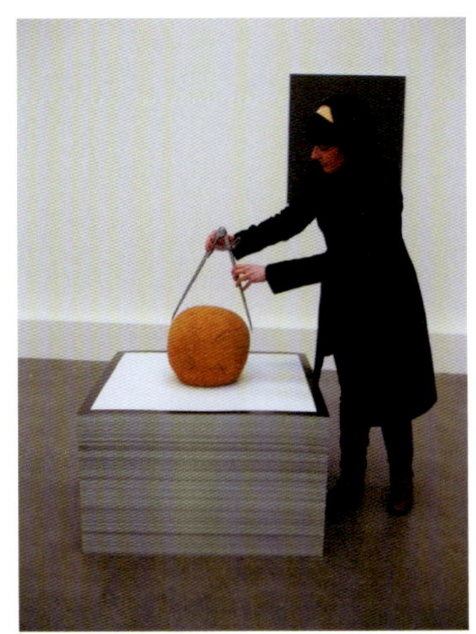

In Roccasalva's work, not only do the images revolve like unresolved specters, but they carry with them the testimonies to their own reality as recorded images that are transmitted and reproduced: as they manifest themselves they also reveal the conditions of their own production. Often they reveal their own reality, which is artificial or a construction like a disguise, as in the case of the faithful reproduction of the photographic error in *The Oval Portrait*, or *The Skeleton Key* (p. 3), in which the painting itself assumes the visual logic of the "plate tectonics" of the cut and paste commands in Photoshop. Despite this, it would be very difficult to speak of an analytical behavior in the art of Pietro Roccasalva, because the moment at which the artifice is pointed out is in no way an end result toward which the work is heading, even if it is a "theme" perpetually treated and absorbed by the work. Here it would be opportune to remember that the title, *The Oval Portrait. A Ventriloquist at a Birthday Party in October 1947*, was literally taken from a famous light box by Jeff Wall, a reference that is in no way random in a discourse on the rules of painterly representation, the manifest artifice, the mise en scène that is exceeded by itself in the same moment that it is exacerbated. All the more so since *The Oval Portrait* is the title of an Edgar Allan Poe story in which the impressive realism that characterizes the portrait of a woman is the result of the interweaving of the painter's obsession with the execution of the painting, and the power itself of that image to come to life by stealing it from its subject.

And it is for this same reason that it is opportune to recall the concept of "meta-pictorial tension" that the art historian Victor I. Stoichita puts forth in his treatment of the moment when the still life shifts from being "peripheral" and marginal to being autonomous in European painting between the end of the 16th century and the second half of the 17th century. At this point in time, what was a subordinate image takes the upper hand over the primary image (the scene with figures and the evangelical story) that it had to support until now as a vulgar, earthly, organic prop. It is the process, thus what is defined as "marginalia"— and carries out the literal function of a disguise—that progresses toward the center of the work and seizes the terrain.

Roccasalva makes an incessant discourse—some would say fabulistic— around painting and representation. This is particularly true when the work does not assume the *technical* form of painting, but rather thematizes it as artifice and cosmetic treatment through the digital print, the tableau vivant, and the installation.

"This 'new' painting genre [the still life] will move forward forming itself out of three fundamental data: [...] the illusionistic representation (in trompe l'œil); the idea of the 'vanity of things'; the meta-pictorial character of the representation."—Victor I. Stoichita, *L'instauration du tableau*[3]

"Illusion," "vanity," and a constant back and forth movement from and toward representation are fundamental concepts within Roccasalva's work, particularly in his superposition of the discourse on painting as a cosmetic treatment for a fundamentally negative conception of existence as a moment of truth; its appearance, the indefatigable preparation of a catastrophic event that would not happen. Or better, in his "situazioni

3
Victor I. Stoichita, *L'instauration du tableau*, Méridien Klincksieck, Paris 1993.

d'opera" (work situations) he seems to want to fit out the stage set and ritual site of an inverse ceremony where a decadent and impoverished idol is celebrated: the collapse of all the systems for producing truth, from philosophy to religion, to science, politics, and the rhetoric of the media. But the instrument of this funereal, yet festive, anticipation is, precisely, the extreme and exacerbated use of the main device through which any ideology is built: the image.

"The still life thematizes [...] the dialectics absence/appearance, truth/illusion, reality/image. It is impossible to understand its birth without considering the reflection on the representation governing it. Since its origins (classic) the still life has put forth its own paradoxical traits, which made it define a sort of 'painterly sophism.'" —Victor I. Stoichita[4]

In this sense, the profoundly skeptical—or should we say cynical?—character of the thought that Pietro Roccasalva's work implicates is expressed through his use of the eccentric and the paradoxical, which are pushed toward the center of the representation from the margins of the moral periphery, as well as through the constant reference to concepts of heresy, corruption, and error.

An example of this procedure of perverting the idea from above may be found in the assimilation of the sun to the "arancino", a typical rice-based Sicilian dish. In his first solo show at Johnen+Schöttle in Cologne, a real, but oversized and abnormal "arancino" (p. 34-35) sat on a ream of paper at the end of the exhibition visit. The black border framing the sheets of paper recalled the graphics of the posters announcing deaths, particularly in central-southern Italy, while the entire ream acted as a base for the kind of extreme trivialization of Lucio Fontana's *Natures*; the perishable quality of the cooked rice hastened the notion of obsolescence and disgust. Visitors to the exhibition were, moreover, invited to have themselves portrayed—as if in a kind of grotesque souvenir of the exhibition—while gripping a compass and measuring the circumference of the "arancino", in a parody of the iconography of Genesis in which the Architect of the World is busy verifying the object of Creation (p. 39). There the measurement of a birth, here the span of a near end. Reinforcing the sense of the funereal derision of the sun was the fact that the entire composition was facing a monochrome canvas, whose dimensions were the same as Giorgione's *Tempesta* (c. 1510); the chromatic painting of its surface was the result of a fantastic projection intent on imagining the result of the fusion of all the colors used in the original of the Renaissance canvas, once time had completed its job corrupting the materials. The entire room offered a series of predictions, from the end of energy to the fossilization of the representation, as well as passing through the collapse of knowledge and memory in their final incarnation: the tourist.

In Ghent, too, at the Hoet Bekaert Gallery, another "arancino" symbolized a sun with an "expiration date" and reigned from its place on the ground, at the center of what was the transposition on the gallery floor of the astral decoration found in Piazza del Campidoglio in Rome (p. 51-52). In other cases, instead—as in the pastel *Untitled* of 2003 (p. 10)—the image of a skull overlaps the image of a small loaf of bread, or better,

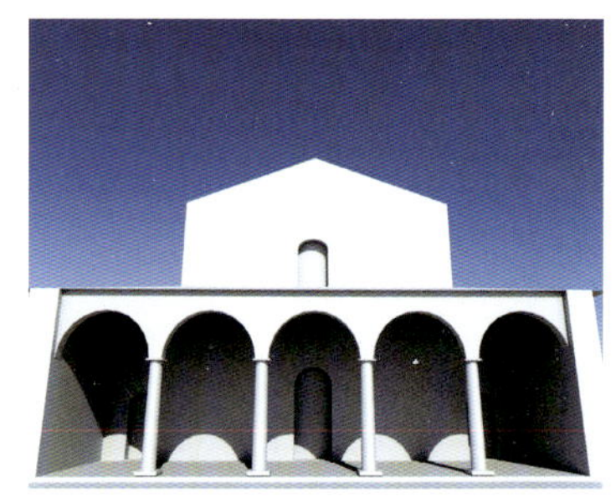

GIOCONDITÀ, 2002

4

Ibid.

metamorphoses into it, as if it were second guessing an inverse transformation process: while in the allegory of the vanitas food (thus the earthly sphere) prefigures death as a collective destiny, here it is the iconography of the memento mori that precipitates in precisely the same allegoric device and oxidizes with the banality.

This assimilation and anticipatory process of the base, the incongruous, and the false, rather than give rise to a series of motives, becomes a modus operandi of the work itself, one of its performative qualities that calls up the function of morphing, a digital technology that is able to metamorphose forms while visualizing the dynamism of the process. This discourse is particularly evident in the recurring motif of the head, as we find it in *Untitled* of 2004, in *The Good Woman* of 2005 (p. 27), or in *The Skeleton Key III* of 2007 (p. 60). Each of these compositions in the form of a portrait—even if the sidereal and alien aspect of these representations makes them seem like corrupt derivations of ancient icons—seems to crystallize an extreme movement: laceration, expulsion, implosion, collapse, oxidation, deglutition, expectoration, contraction, spasm, and prolapse. Although they are unique and coherent images, they seem to preserve the memory of the different studies and sketches that produce them, as if fragments, angulations, and attempts that are different from one another, and spurious, have found a momentary and precarious point of fusion.

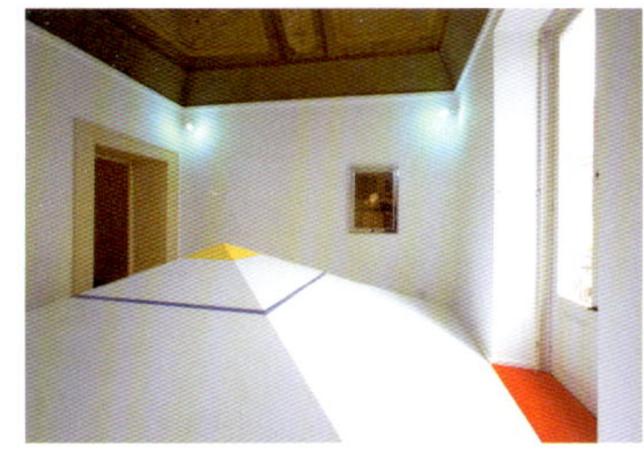

FISHEYE, 2003

In their obvious state as "synthetic" images—meaning they are the result of a synthesis and thus artificial—these heads make clear their assimilation of an entire history of painting, a history that bears the hallmark of the decomposition of the parts and their inadequate reintegration, of the incongruous combination and the psychic and sexual friction, of the compression of forms and their release as scattered parts. It is a story that ranges from Dadaist derision because of proportion and coherence to the frenzy of Surrealist coitus between men, animals, and things, and that traverses the continuous dissection and reinvention of form in the work of Picasso, to arrive at Bacon, at the constant postponement of the moment in which the missing parts will be reintegrated among themselves. But Roccasalva's is not an operation on the eclecticism of styles nor on the emptying of the historic meanings. His is more of an operation on the mobility of the vision and the need to disconnect images from the predications of truth, through constant recourse to deceit, simulation, and artifice. In fact, when he talks about his own work he often uses a metaphor related to technology for shooting and broadcasting photographic, cinematographic, or electronic images, often implicating the lens—as he literally does in *Fisheye* (2003)—surveillance, and projection mechanisms as obvious extensions of the watchful eye, of the recorded object, of reproducible time, and of the gaze as a relationship of power and subjugation (p. 12-13).

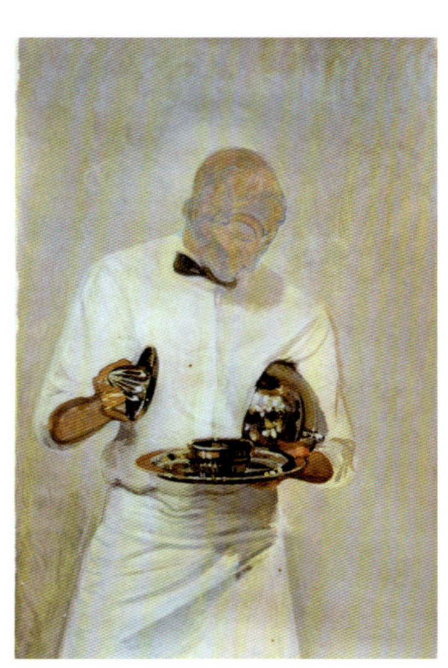

UNTITLED, 2005

Most of all, the video image and the picture have often been used as extreme poles of the same discourse on movement, in work situations where the picture found itself at the end of a tour that included the moving image as a transitory moment. In his solo shows at Viafarini in Milan (2004), Johnen+Schöttle in Cologne (2006), and GAMeC in Bergamo (2007), the picture (and above all the recurring motif of heads) was collocated at the arrival point of itineraries in which different stages of stagnation and dynamism were represented as successive stages, using as many media. In this paradoxical inversion of the very idea of movement—in which the video image corresponds to the fixity of the loop while the picture image incorporates instability and transformation—the different techniques for tableaux vivants and sculpture become "latent" stages of the picture. They are always part of a constellation of elements in which the discourse on the representation and on the need for an iconographic production is spatialized and dramatized. In his installation approach to painting, it is in this form of dramatization of the objects arranged in the space that the references to the ephemeral apparatus of the baroque and to the allegorical function of 17th-century still lifes converge, as do certain affinities with the iconographic politics of objects among artists such as Thomas Schutte, Katharina Fritsch, Gino De Dominicis, or Robert Gober, and even artists that are closer to Roccasalva from a generational perspective, such as Sterling Ruby and Victor Man. From a certain point of view the diversity of this series of examples is related to an idea of image as head, and as a depository of codes, memories, and conventions that have been stratified over time, while from another perspective, it reveals operative modes that are radically different with regard to the images themselves: from the articulation of the combinatory practice to the extreme synthesis of the icon. And while on the one hand Roccasalva's images are sediments that are extremely rich with erudite and punctual references—according to an idea that history and tradition are like a labyrinth of dark areas and cyclically operative heresies—on the other his personal methodology seems to sometimes work "against" the mere idea of iconography and the production of images. The recurring motif of food, for example, is often treated as deterioration or assimilated to digestion and expulsion, as in the case of the sun symbolized by the "arancino" or by the approximation of the skull to bread, almost a retaliation of the memento mori, a reversal of the vanitas that, expulsed from the dominion of moral allegory, reconquers the sphere of banality. Or the same motif of the gaze as a moment of understanding that becomes anatomic inspec-tion. In fact, if we think again about *Jockey Full of Bourbon*, we may note how the spectator peeks through a small pastel at an owl disguised as a parrot, or an animal that in classical iconography is a symbol of omni-science, but that in this instance assumes the appearance of a bird which, when consulted, cannot answer but merely repeats the question asked. But what is interesting is that this process of perverting the philosophical interrogation and the dignity of belief reduced to simulation occurs within two adjoining rooms that were previously lavatories and today still have some of their sanitary fittings, while the hole in the drawing on the wall that allows the spectator to see the other half of the instal-lation becomes an orifice, as if it were an extreme and grotesque intestinal version of Marcel Duchamp's *Étant donnés*.

The theme of the moving image as a degenerating phase of the gaze is central in *Truka*, Roccasalva's solo show at GAMeC in Bergamo (p. 58–60). Here the installation was made up of three elements that revolved around the artist's personal remake of Andrei Tarkovsky's *Andrei Rublev*. In the prologue to the 1969 film, a peasant attempts to fly in a hot air balloon, only to crash to the grassy ground a few minutes later. The camera

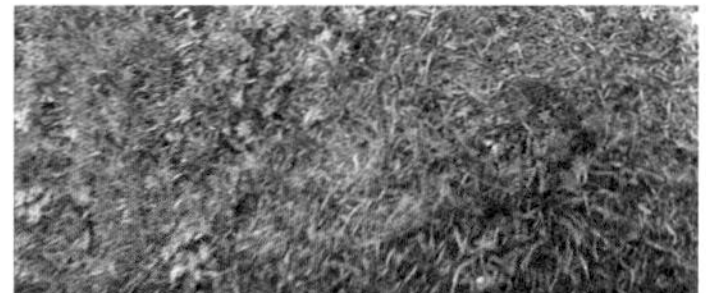
ANDREI TARKOVSKY, *ANDREI RUBLEV*, 1966

follows the ruinous movement in a subjective shot and the balloon comes
to rest, ending the sequence with a still of the field. The latter was
realized using a technical artifice called "truka," from the machine that
was once used to produce visual effects during the editing phase that
were otherwise irreproducible during the filming. Roccasalva's remake
consists of extending this single photogram to the entire length of the
prologue, the soundtrack of which plays on, unchanged: the image is
thus disconnected from the flow of the narrative and the projection of
the 35 mm is reduced to the contemplation of a kind of technical breakdown,
almost as if the protagonist's arrested fall had backwardly infected the
integrity of the film's support preceding it. The sculpture and the painting
that complete the installation, meanwhile, synthesize different moments
and outcomes of a same descending movement. *Clinamen II* consists
of an enormous wig whose colors suggest a flame, and is in the shape of
the comet in Giotto's *Adoration of the Magi*; but Roccasalva's follows an
inverted (upward) movement and is halted in an improbable ascension,
rendered by the state of maximum flexion of the structure from which the
wig hangs—the equipment used for pole jumping—frozen at the moment
of maximum tension, just before the athlete is catapulted from the ground.
The picture entitled *The Skeleton Key III*, meanwhile, portrays the face of
an elevator operator, a figure that recurs in several works, who is placed
like a kind of guardian of the cyclic dynamism, like a mechanical Sisyphus
caught in a perpetual up and down movement. A witness to the transformation that, in his own disarticulated physiognomy, incorporates the
fall and the impact, the deflagration of the vision that runs from Pointillism
to Cubism, the distortion of the dispersed and mismanaged physiognomy
that reaches from Arcimboldo to Bacon and the cut and paste of Photoshop,
the entropy of the syntax that animates the Constructivist collage and the
"traumatic realism" of postmodern bodies.

The center of this syncopated narration of rise and fall is the film,
characterized by dilated error: it is this negative, depressed, and depres-
sive moment of the vision as a disturbance and a whirlpool, like quicksand,
that works like the eye of the storm of what the artist himself defines as
"an ultimate, apocalyptic *déjeuner sur l'herbe*," in which the painting
and the sculpture are respectively the spectator and "spectatrice" who
are called upon to watch this auto-implosion of the moving image.

Presenting itself as constitutionally eccentric, the work of Roccasalva
offers itself in a programmatic manner as an object of refuse. It anticipates
the simulation and ideology, and in doing so puts the spectator in a state
of alert, just as it seduces and cajoles his senses.

In his work, the images of truth and the symbols of the metaphysical are
confused with the grotesque figures from bawdy theater, and interroga-
tions about the meaning of existence collide with profanation and negation.
In its eccentricity with respect to today's news, Roccasalva's work seems
to reveal a project that it would be appropriate to call political in a
paradoxical manner because it tends toward a form of hyperbolic freedom:
or more precisely, the perversion and the decay of the systems that
produce truth and of the parameters for communication, through the extreme
maturation of deceit and the idol.

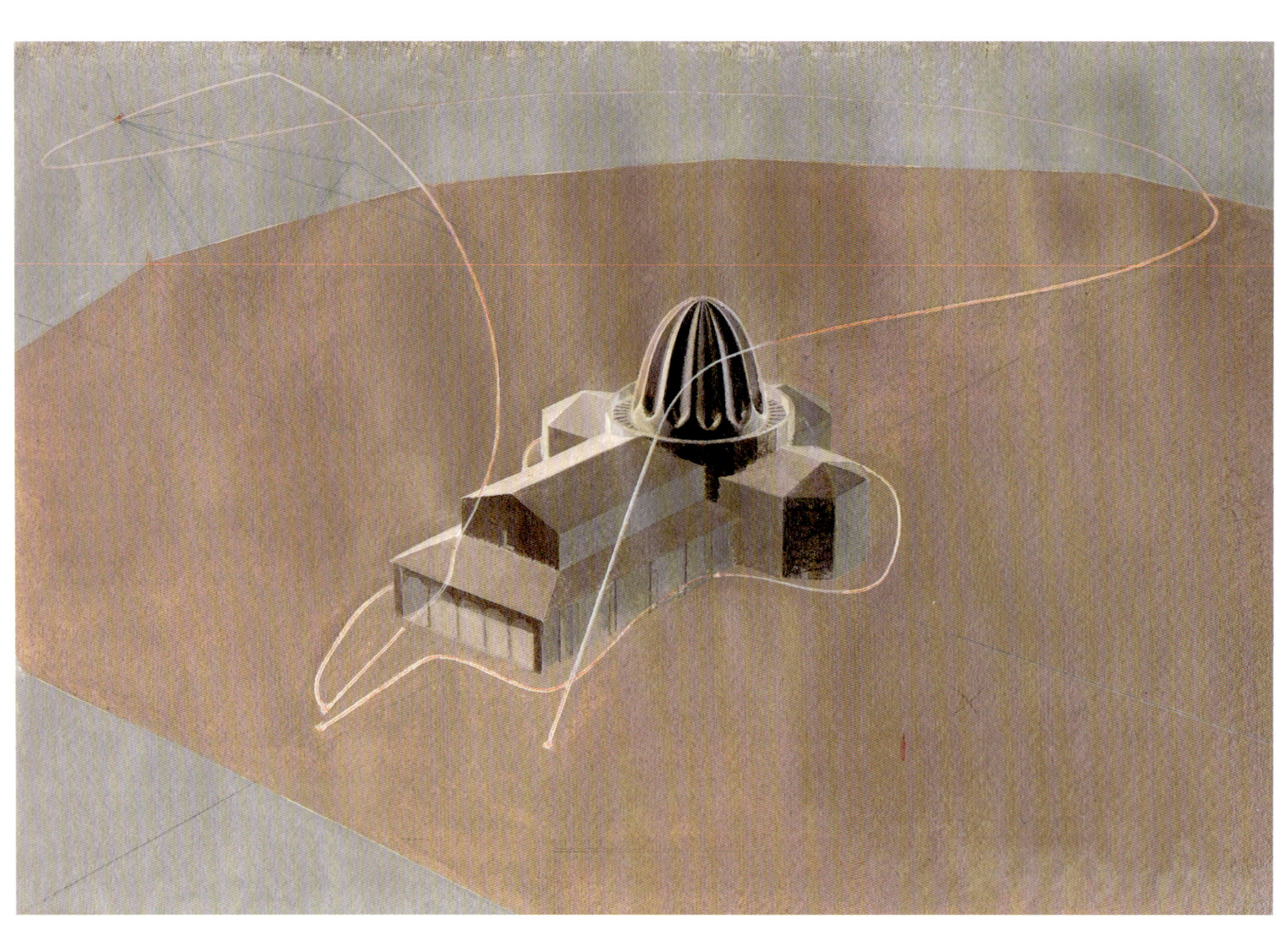

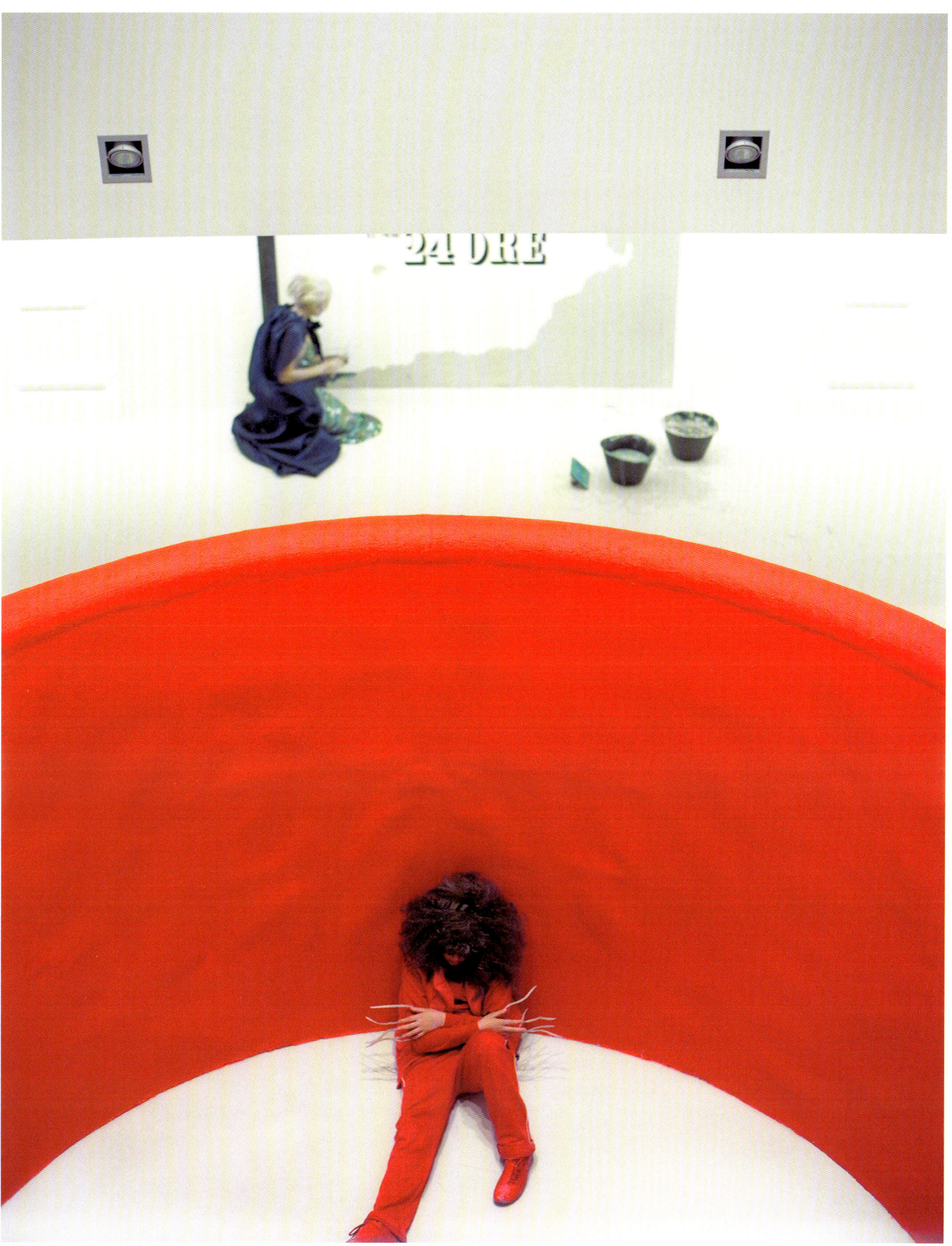

Exhibition view *My Private #4*, 2006

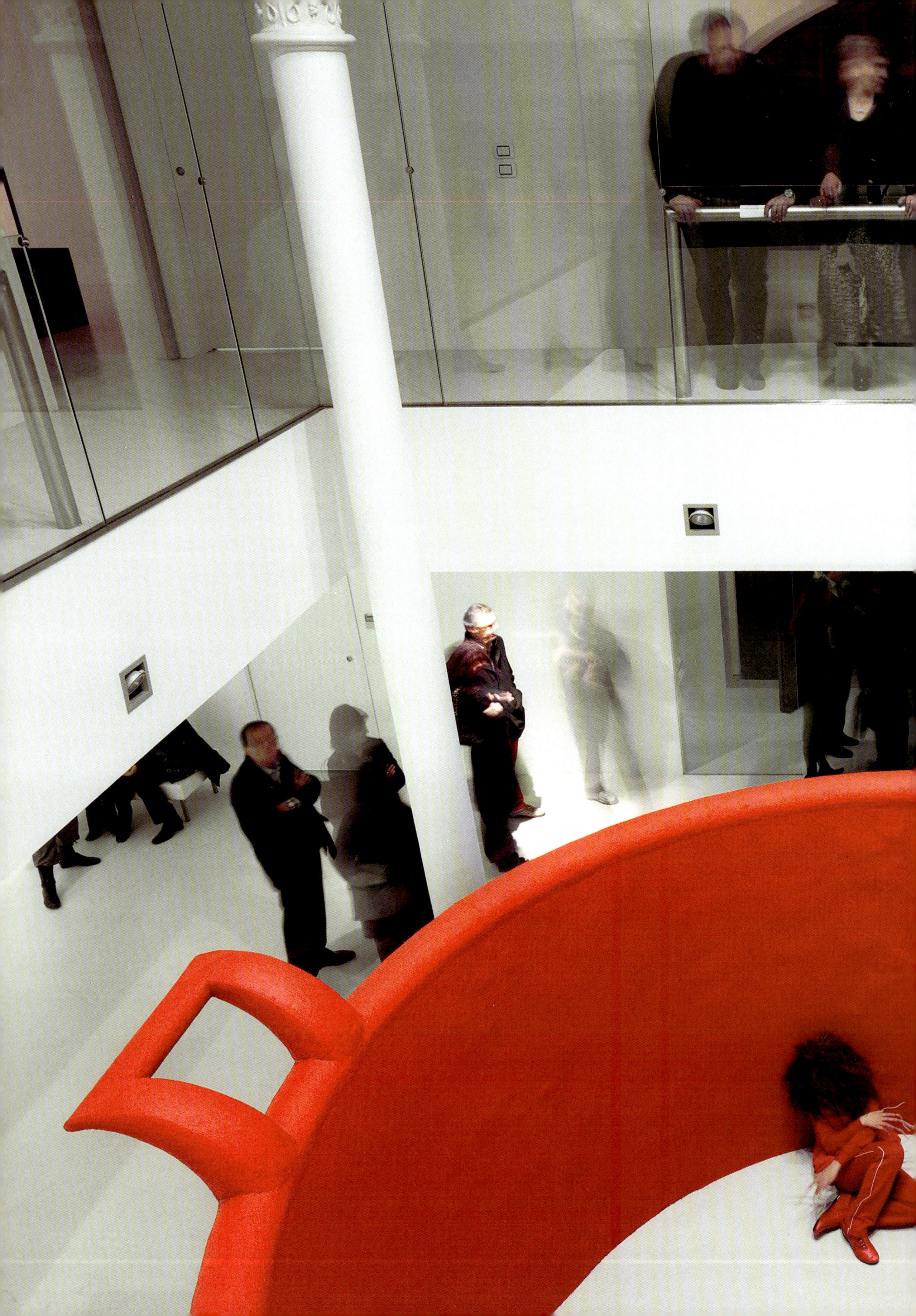

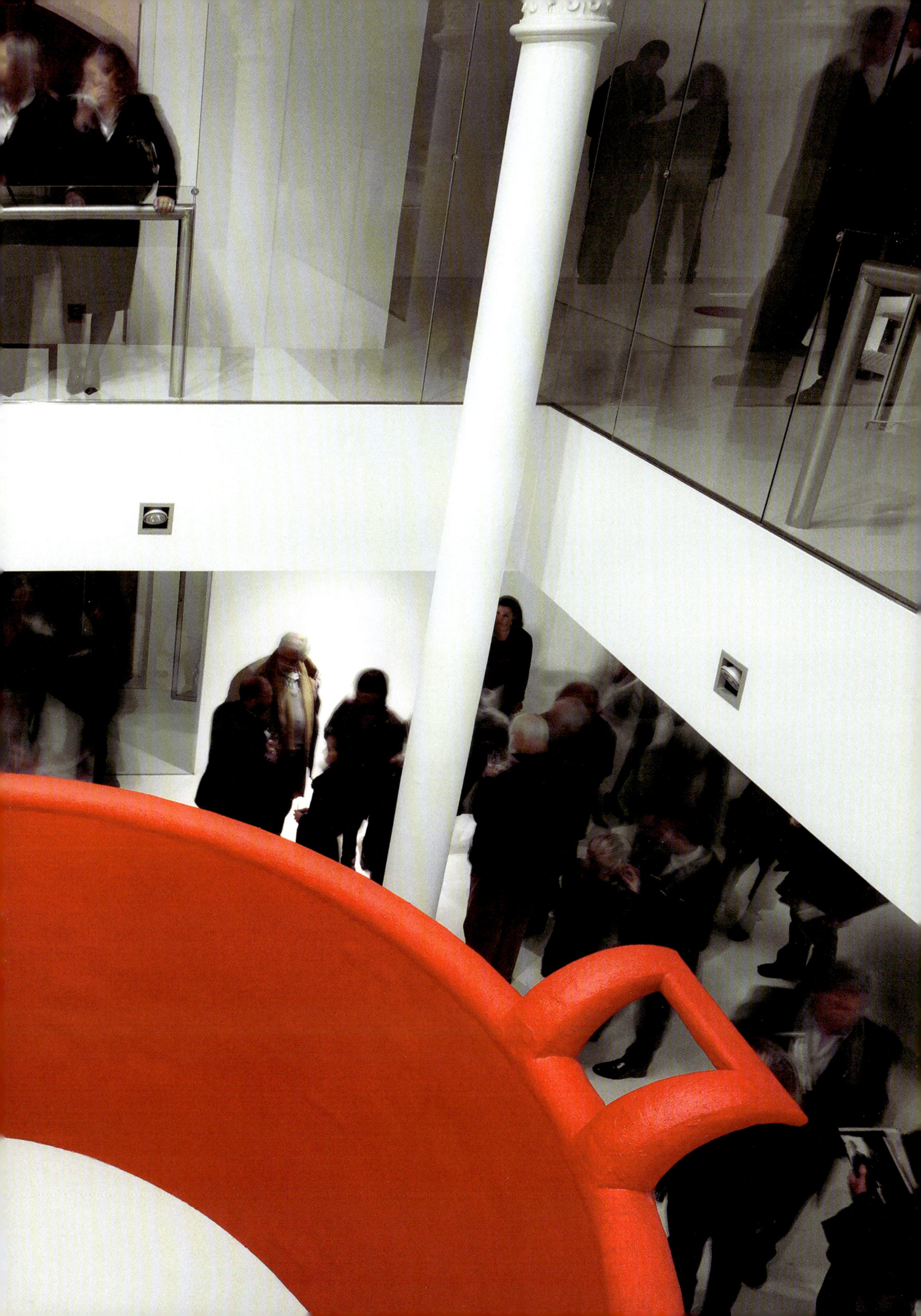

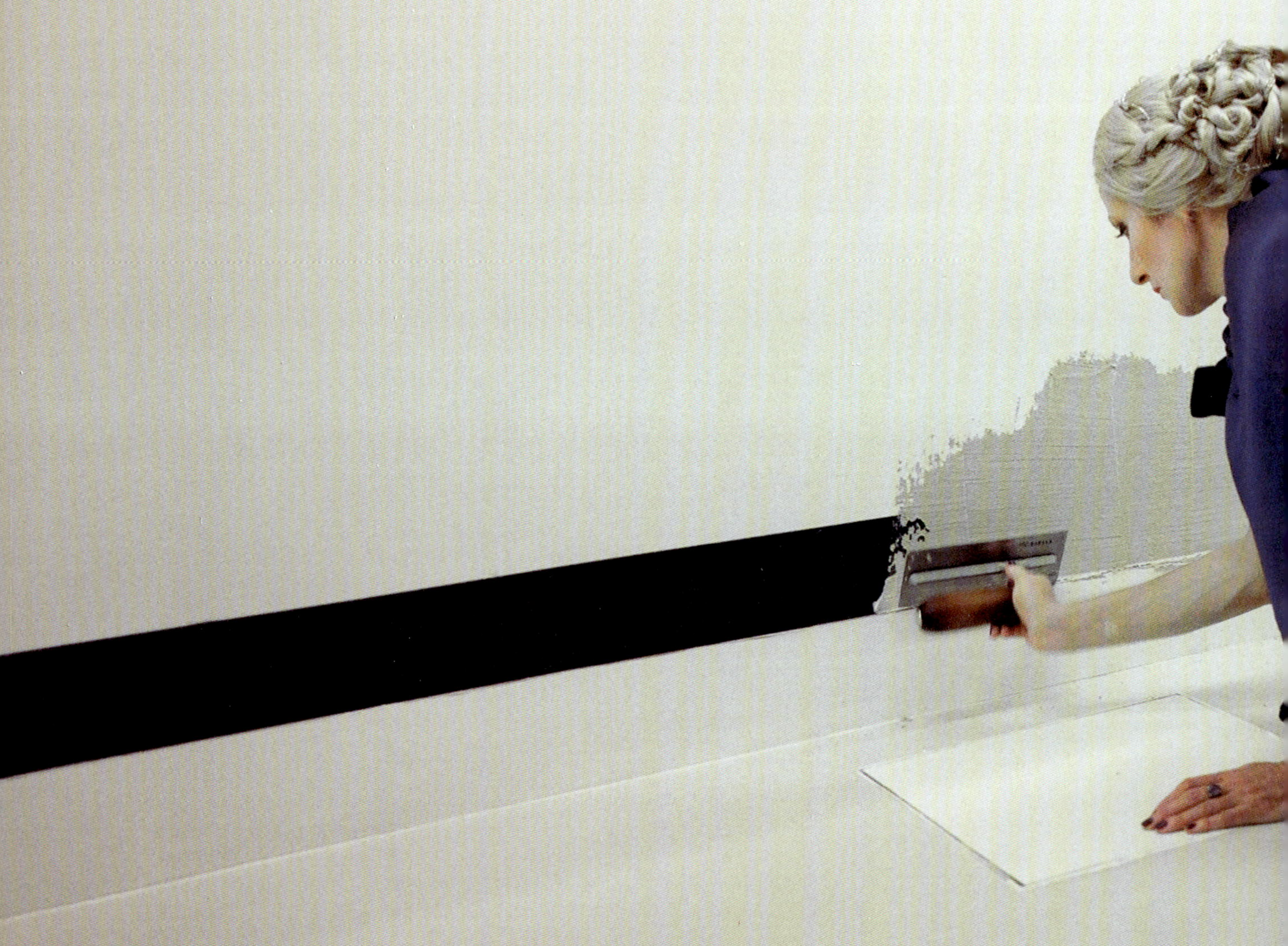
Il Sole 24 ORE

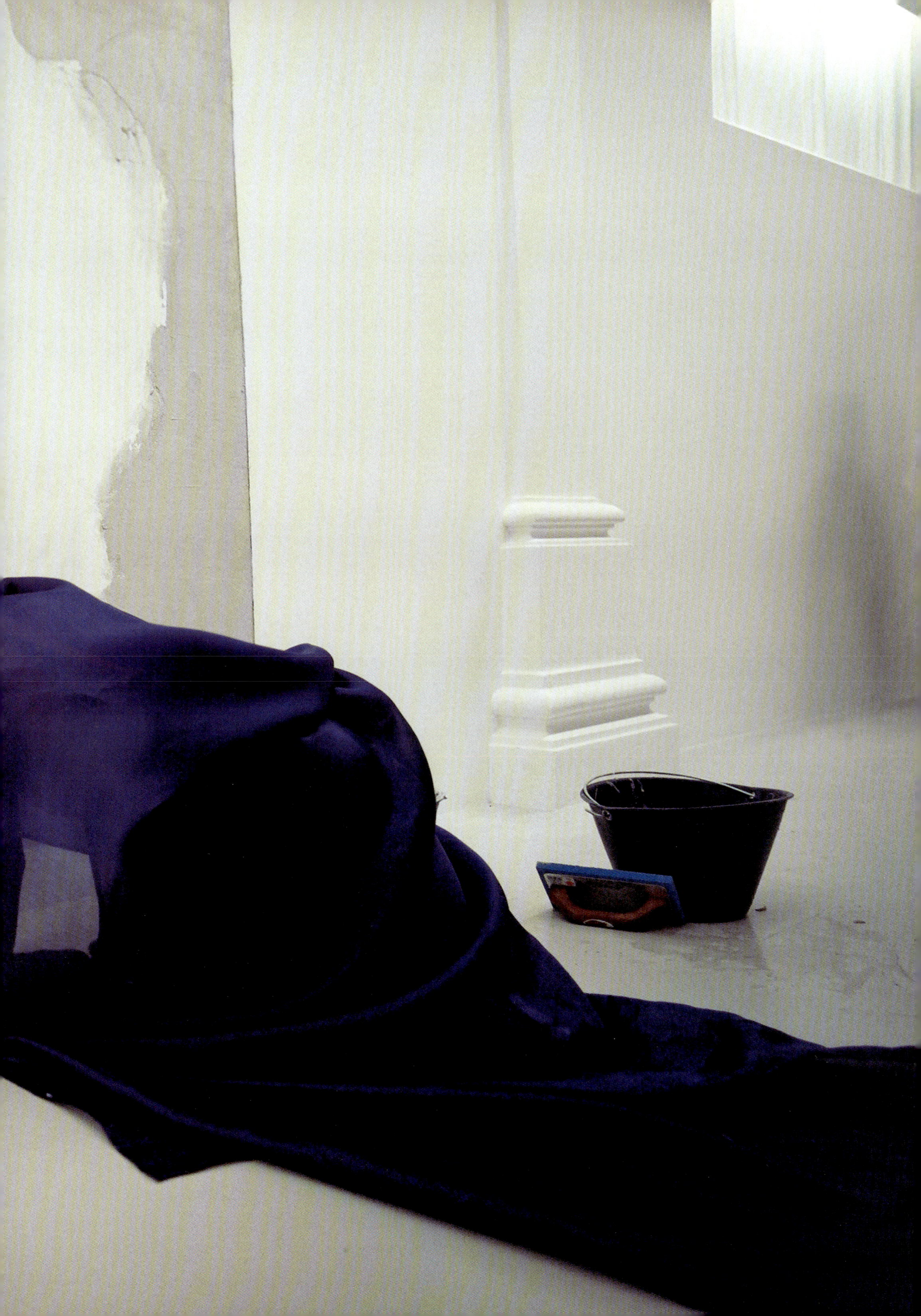

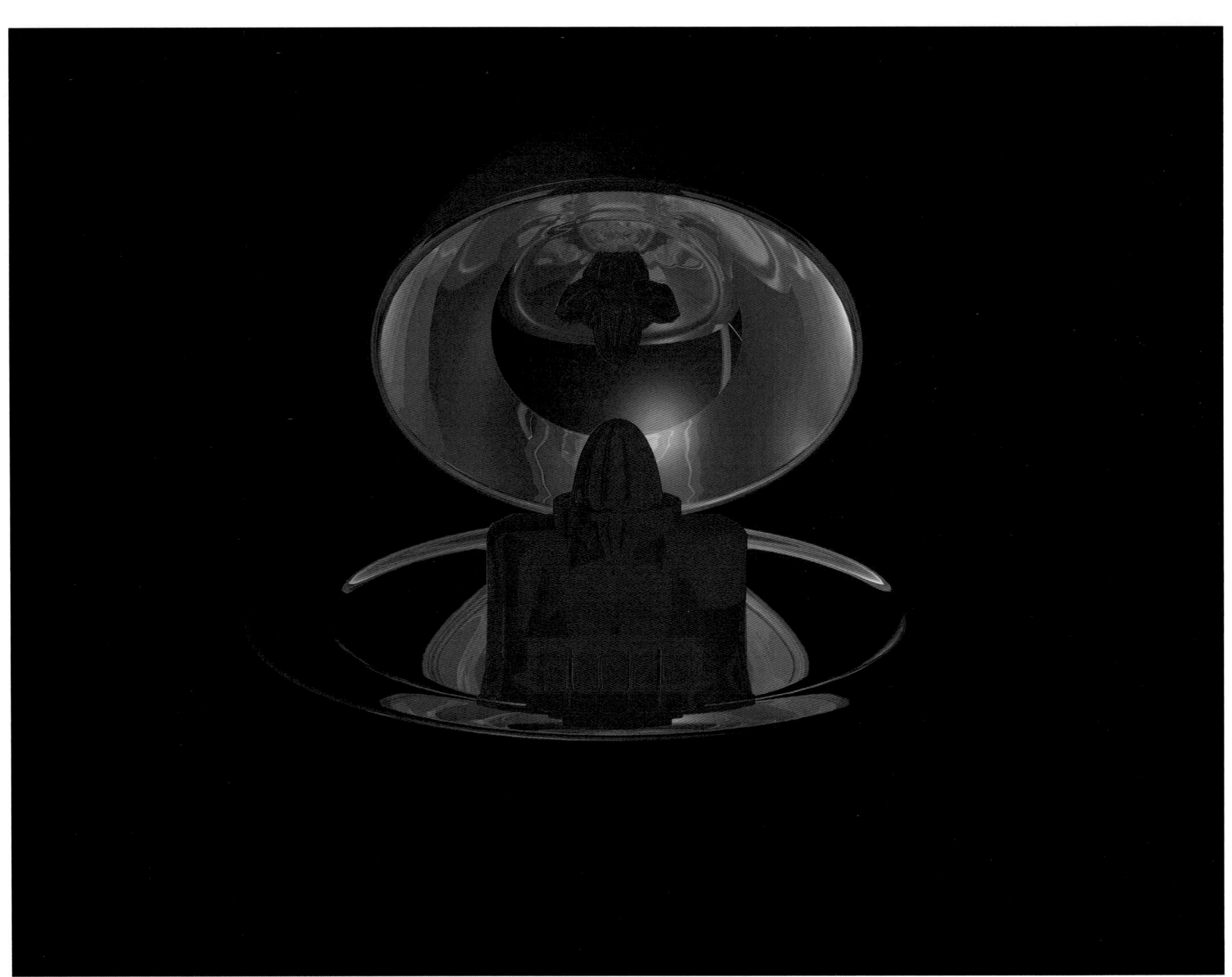

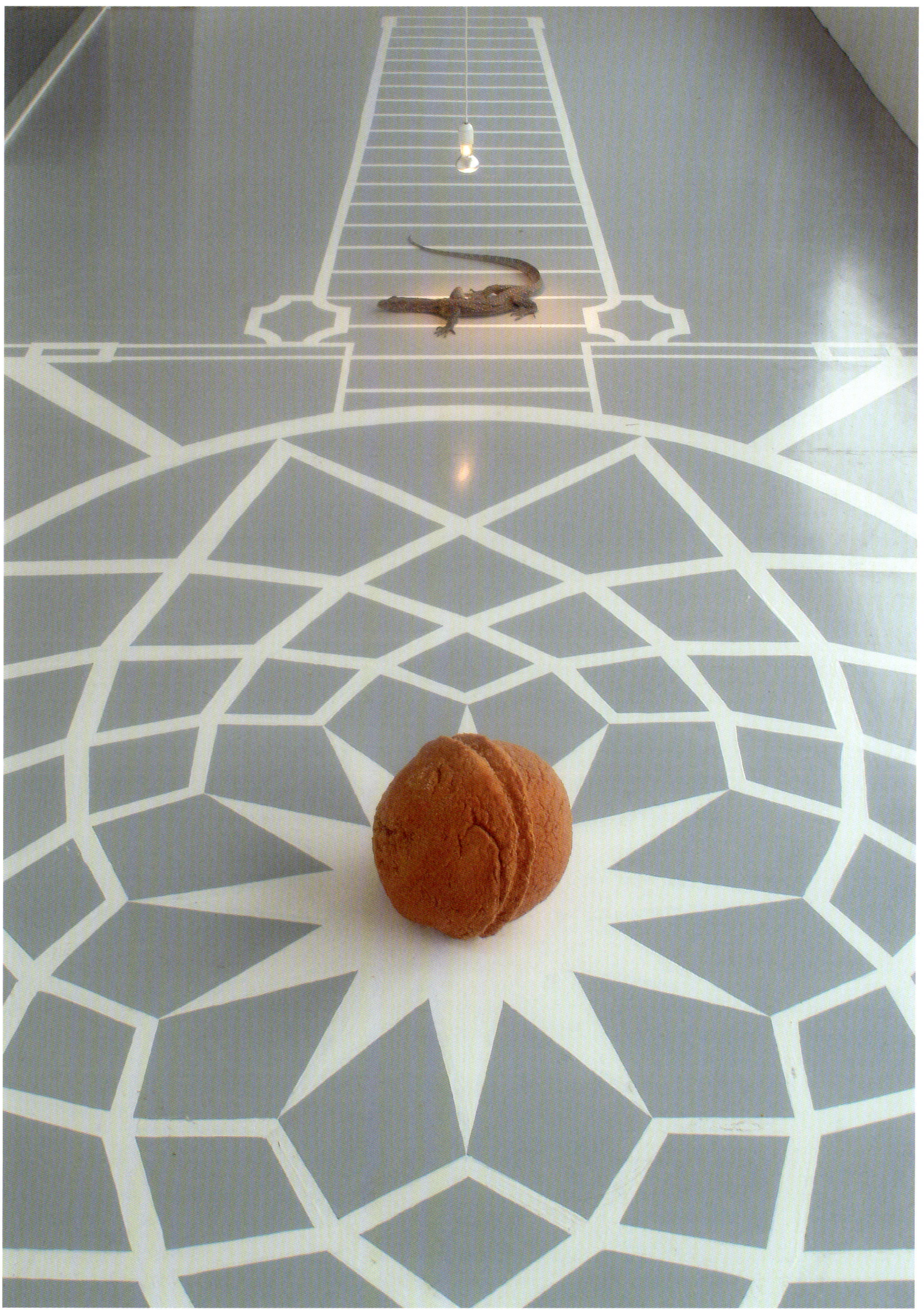

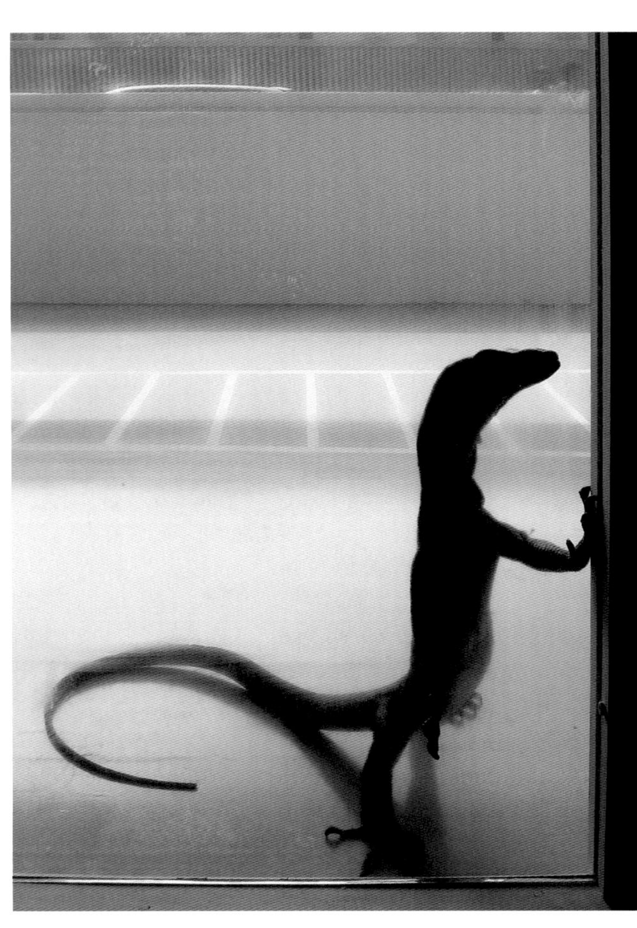

Interview
Edoardo Gnemmi

EDOARDO GNEMMI Was there a specific moment when you decided to become an artist?

PIETRO ROCCASALVA No, art is a kind of possession.

EDOARDO GNEMMI Your works are often born out of a relationship with their predecessors, they are self-generating, as if they were part of a closed, self-sufficient system. Some of your painterly works in particular appear to almost subdue reality. An important presupposition is the concept of the "situazione d'opera"—the work situation—can you tell me about this?

PIETRO ROCCASALVA The worksite is a cathedral that operates like a bachelor machine, a mill that grinds the time away. The paintings are the microchips, the processors; the "situazione d'opera" is the range of action of a painting as an "intelligent artifice" or simulacrum.

EDOARDO GNEMMI Thus different elements and languages always cohabit with one or more paintings. Is it a kind of great collage?

PIETRO ROCCASALVA It is the extreme implication of collage. It is excess. The collage, which is born as an "impure" practice that includes fragments of contextual reality within the picture, is now complete and exceeded through the inverse process that includes the "pure" element of the picture in this kind of expanded collage.

EDOARDO GNEMMI Might one say that your pictures have a memory?

PIETRO ROCCASALVA If they ever had one, it would be the memory of a journey to oblivion. The paintings are the centrifuge of the image, the open mouth, and the whirlpool in the flux of the worksite. The iconography is gradually forgotten rather than remembered: for what remains, much disappears, while new elements that push the others into the same abyss through the picture enter into play.

EDOARDO GNEMMI In this mise-en-abîme, is there no risk that the next work will demote the previous work to the role of a means rather than an end?

PIETRO ROCCASALVA No, because there is no distinction between *ergon* and *parergon*, the work and the context chase one another, changing roles, making them both the means and the end simultaneously.

EDOARDO GNEMMI Edgar Degas said that it is always necessary to correct, to never complete work. What roles do failure and error play in your works?

PIETRO ROCCASALVA My works are bouquets of errors.

EDOARDO GNEMMI For you painting is a fixed point, a stasis and stopping, the only moment when the process undergoes total and terminal crystallization. Your non-painterly works, instead, are instable from a certain viewpoint, conditioned by a time factor—I'm thinking of tableaux vivants, videos, neons, the rice "arancino."

PIETRO ROCCASALVA All these elements are autonomous phases in a process that uses painting as its starting and end point. Painting is the immobile residue of development that traverses the other languages in a "backward" process of stages, from the more fluid to the more crystallized. By shifting the vantage point, what remains outside the picture is another kind of "left over" that will be recycled in some way. The problem of the "left over" is fundamental.

EDOARDO GNEMMI Will this development involving continuous becoming ever find a definitive arrival point, a conclusion?

PIETRO ROCCASALVA Yes. The picture will expand from the center of the collage, recapitulating all the elements: the victory of the sun over the sun in a great still life as the sum of the remains and degeneration of the major genres.

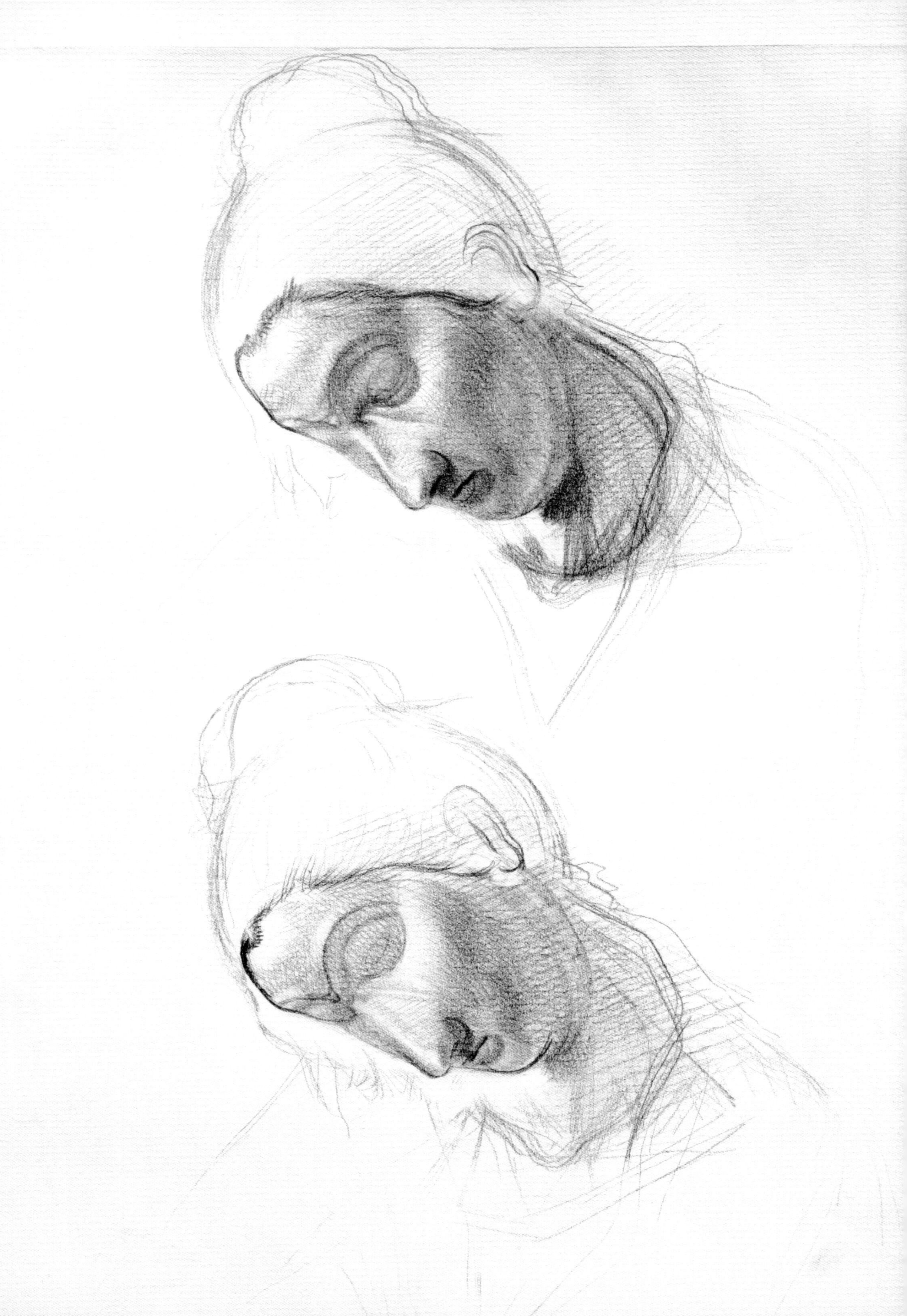

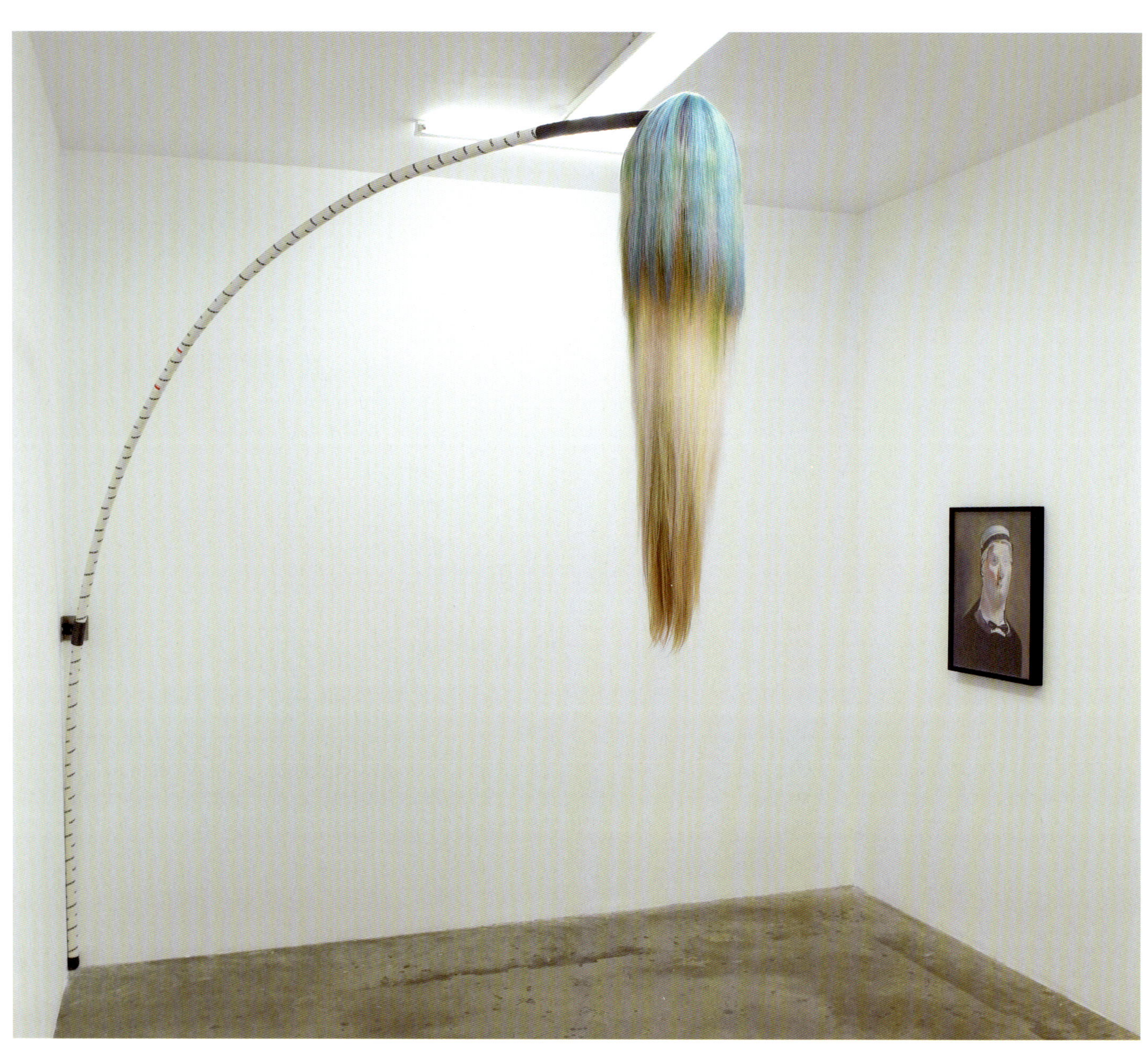

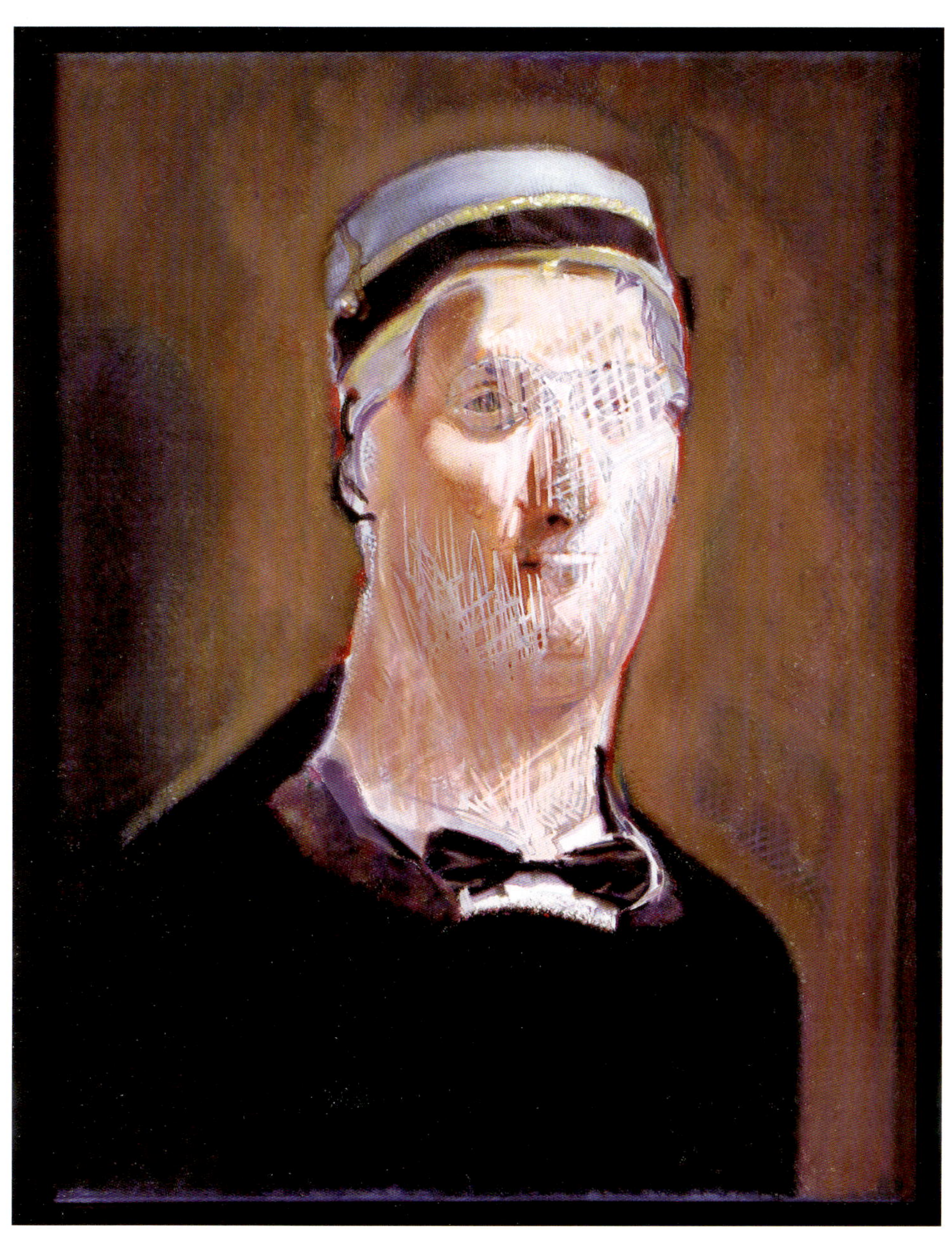

THE SKELETON KEY II, 2007

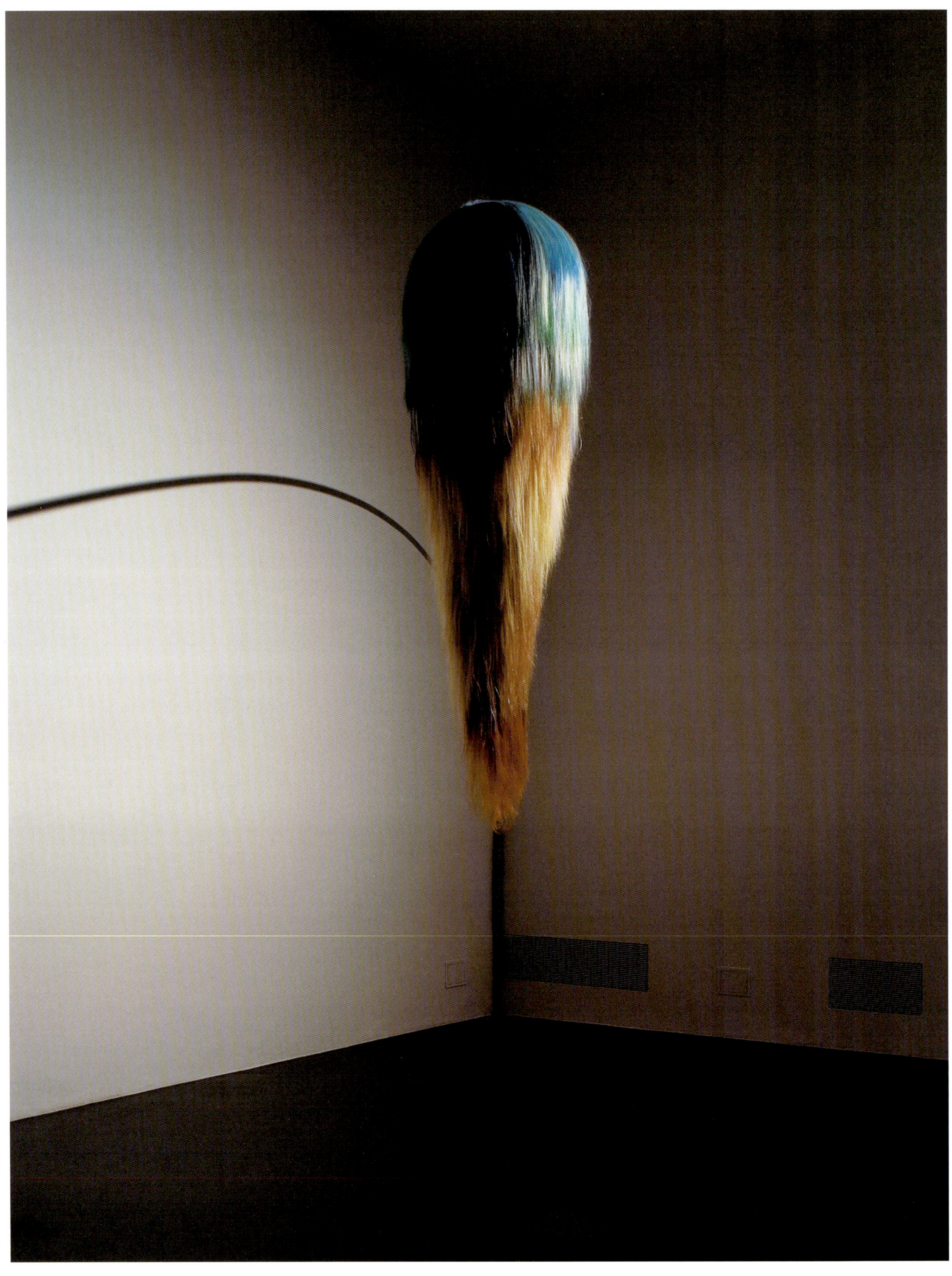

CLINAMEN II, 2007

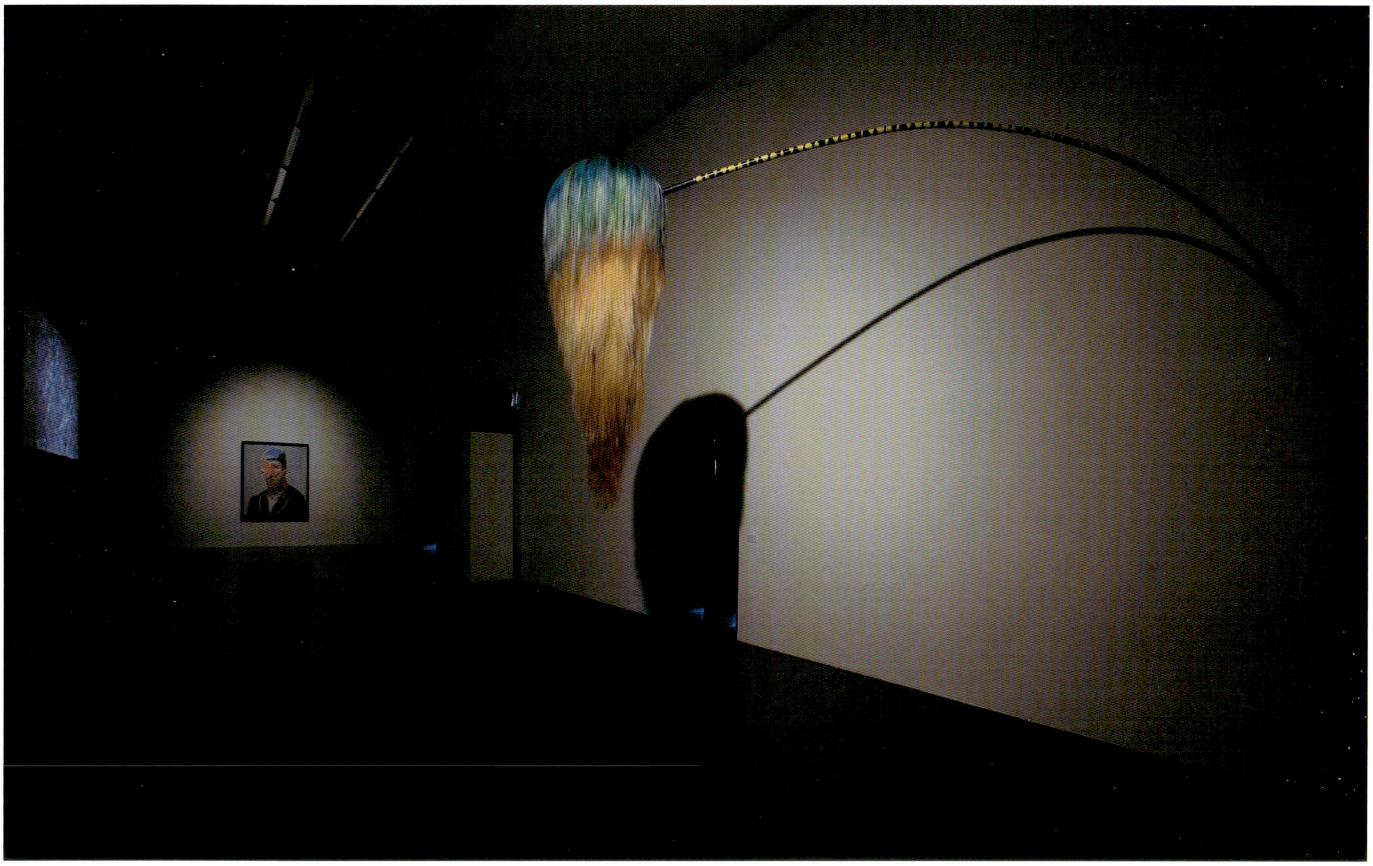

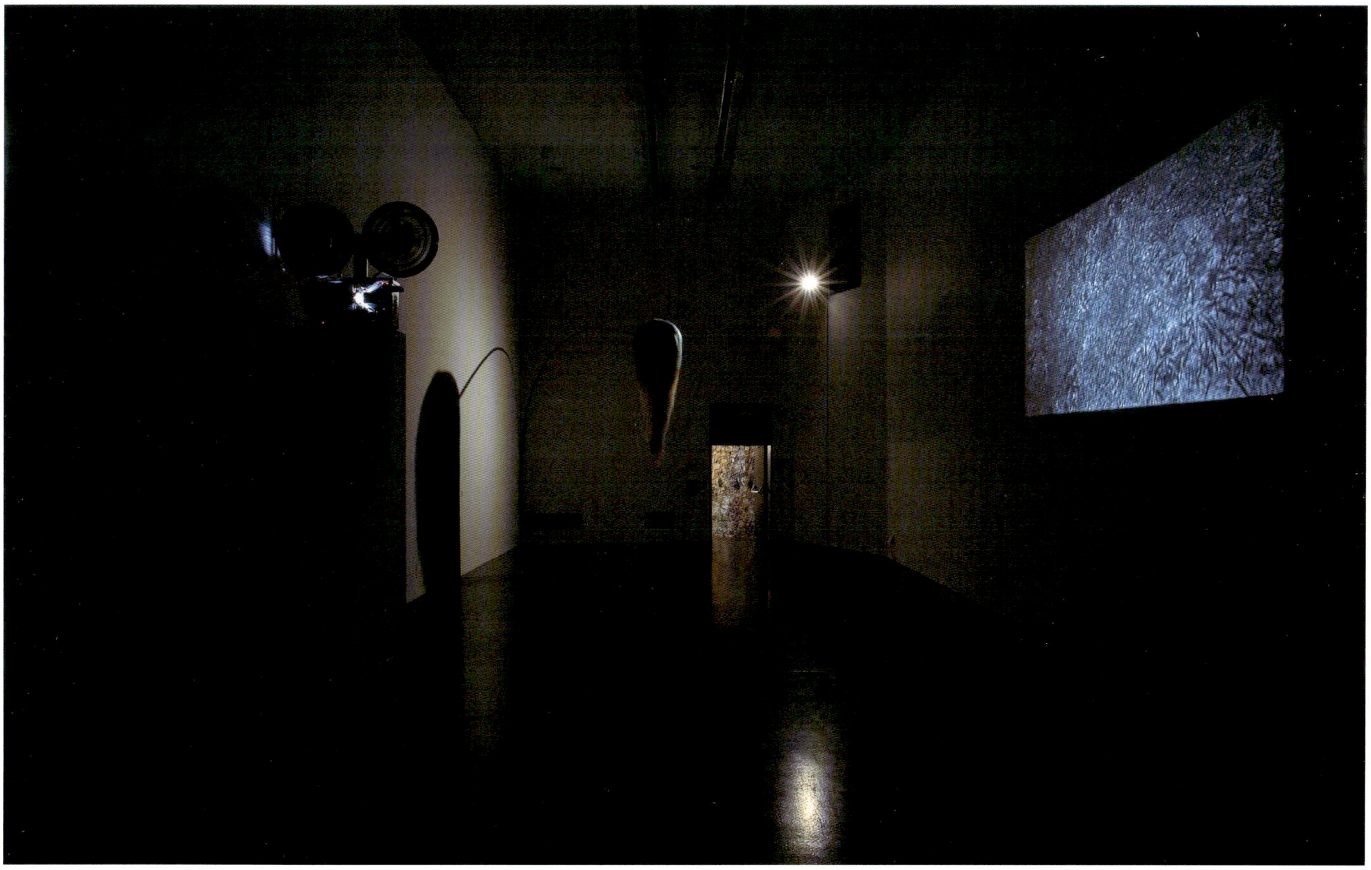

Exhibition view *Truka*, 2007

→
THE SKELETON KEY III, 2007

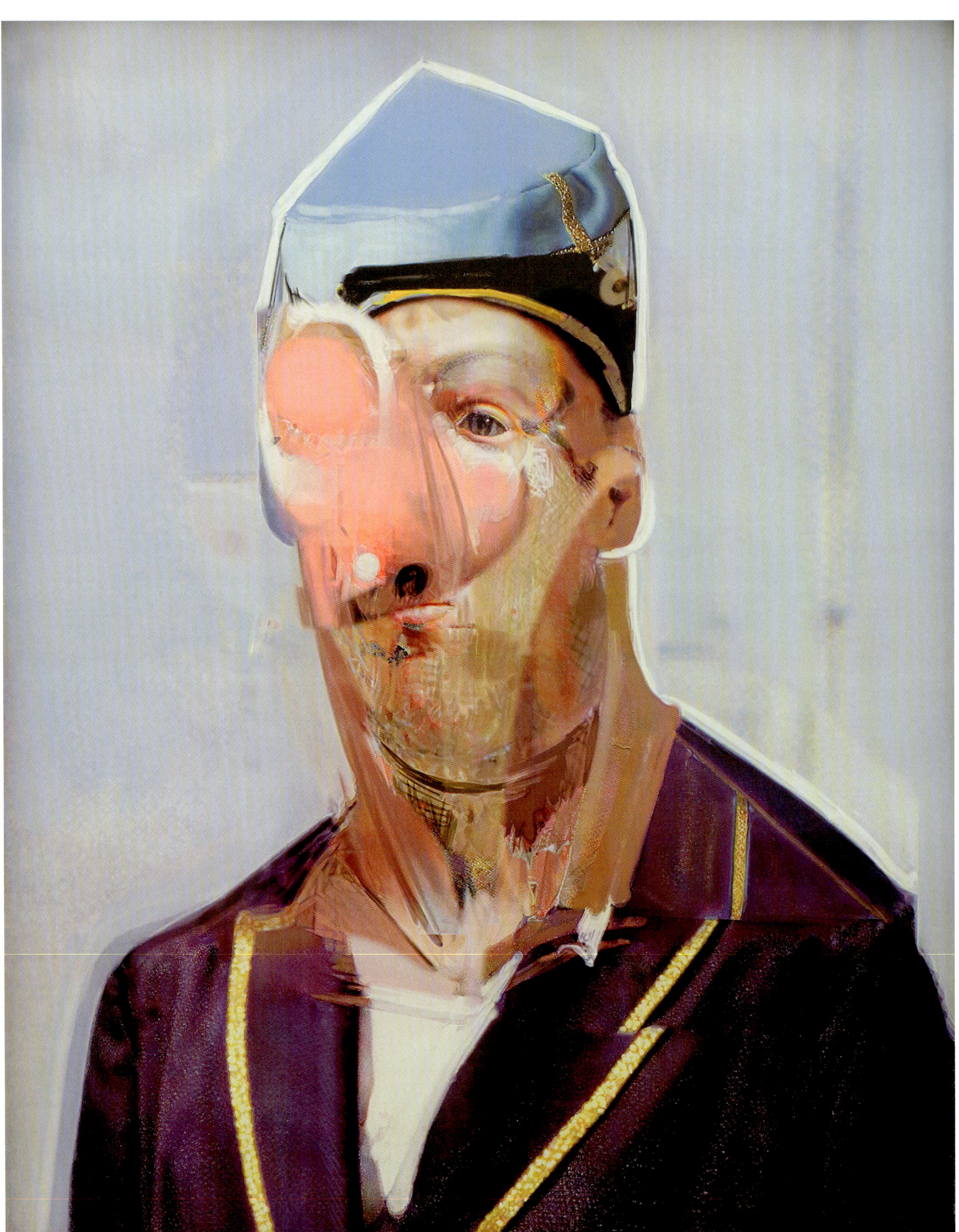

Born 1970, Modica, Italy. Lives and works in Milan.

SOLO EXHIBITIONS
2008
 Z, in "High Resolution: Artists Projects at the Armory,"
 CCS Bard at Park Avenue Armory, New York City, USA
 Art Statements, Art 39 Basel, Basel, Switzerland
2007
 Truka, GAMeC-Galleria d'Arte Moderna e Contemporanea,
  Bergamo; Galleria Civica Montevergini, Siracusa, Italy
 Truka, art: concept, Paris, France
2006
 Il Traviatore, Fondazione Querini Stampalia, Venice, Italy
 My Private #4, Ex Tempio Metodista, Turin, Italy
 De Morgen, Hoet Bekaert Gallery, Ghent, Belgium
 La Tempesta, Johnen+Schöttle, Cologne, Germany
2005
 Ø, ZERO..., Milan, Italy
 ARCO-Project room Hoet Bekaert Gallery (Ghent),
  Madrid, Spain
2004
 O.H., Viafarini, Milan, Italy
2003
 Fisheye, Vistamare, Pescara, Italy

SELECTED GROUP EXHIBITIONS
2008
 In Geneva No One Can Hear You Scream, Blondeau Fine Art
  Services, Geneva, Switzerland
 Manifesta 7, Trentino–South Tyrol, Italy
 Italics; Arte Italiana fra Tradizione e Rivoluzione, 1968–2008,
  Palazzo Grassi, Venice, Italy
2007
 Solo24Ore, MUSEION–Museo d'Arte Moderna e
  Contemporanea, Bolzano, Italy
 Senso Unico, P.S.1, New York City, USA
 A gap in keeping silent: noise, Poetry Summer Watou,
  Poëziezomers, Watou, Belgium
 Apocalittici e Integrati. Ventiquattro artisti italiani, MAXXI,
  Rome, Italy
 Camera con vista, Palazzo Reale, Milan, Italy
 PRAGUE Biennale 3, Prague, Czech Republic
2006
 Partoftheprocess2, ZERO..., Milan, Italy
 PAINTING CODES: i codici della pittura, Galleria Comunale
  d'Arte Contemporanea, Monfalcone (GO), Italy
 *La Città di Leonardo, L'arte Contemporanea, Milano e
  Leonardo*, Fondazione Stelline, Milan, Italy
2005
 Follow my Shadow, Premio Furla per l'Arte, Villa delle Rose,
  Bologna, Italy
 Strata. Difference and Repetition, Fondazione Davide
  Halevim, Milan, Italy
 Changes of mind: Belief and Transformation, Haunch
  Venison, London, UK
 Generation of Art-10 anni alla FAR, Fondazione Antonio
  Ratti, Como, Italy
 XIV Quadriennale di Roma, Galleria Nazionale d'Arte
  Moderna, Rome, Italy
2004
 Partoftheprocess, ZERO..., Milan, Italy
 Paradiso Inferno, Fondazione Bevilacqua La Masa,
  Venice, Italy
2003
 Tracce di un seminario, Viafarini, Milan, Italy
 Opening, Beaulieu Art Gallery, Ghent, Belgium
 II Tirana Biennale, Tirana, Albania
 Forse Italia, S.M.A.K., Ghent, Belgium
 Great Expectations!, "Fuori Uso", Pescara, Italy
2002
 La Riproriduzione, Istituto Nazionale per la Grafica e la
  Calcografia, Rome; Archivio di Stato, Turin, Italy
 *In Extremis, Advanced Course in Visual Arts (with Giulio
  Paolini)*, Fondazione Antonio Ratti, Como, Italy

SELECTED BIBLIOGRAPHY
2008
 In Geneva No One Can Hear You Scream, exhibition
  catalogue, Blondeau Fine Art Services, Geneva,
  JRP|Ringier, Zurich
2007
 A gap in keeping silent: noise, exhibition catalogue,
  Poëziezomer 07, Watou, Belgium
 Manfrin, Paola, "Roccasalva at GAMeC, Bergamo,"
  L'Uomo Vogue, no. 381, May–June, p. 80
 Savaris, Marta, "Pietro Roccasalva," *Flash Art*,
  no. 262, February–March, p. 127
 Lissoni, Andrea, "Questione di fantasmi(ni)," *Rolling Sone*,
  no. 40, February, p. 165
 Hoet, Jan, "The Ark of Pietro Roccasalva," *Janus*, no. 21,
  January, p. 46–53
 Bonvicini, Gyonata, "Pietro Roccasalva," *Flash Art
  International*, no. 252, January–February, p. 113
2006
 Gioni, Massimiliano, "On the ground—Milan," *Artforum*,
  no.4, December, p. 259–261
 Casavecchia, Barbara, "Pietro Roccasalva. Opera e fuori-
  opera," *Flash Art*, no. 261, December 2006–January
  2007, p. 98–101
 "Pietro Roccasalva," curated by My Private, *MOUSSE
  Magazine*, no. 4, November, p. 73
 "My Private n°4: Pietro Roccasalva," *Flash Art*, no. 260,
  October–November, p. 66
 Poli, Francesco, "Roccasalva in privato. A Torino," *Arte*,
  no. 399, November, p. 202
 Rabottini, Alessandro, "Pietro Roccasalva," *Tema Celeste*,
  no. 118, November–December, p. 114
 Della Casa, Bettina, "Pietro Roccasalva," *Temporale*,
  no. 62–63, Eizioni Studio Dabbeni, p. 34–39
 My Private#4—Pietro Roccasalva, exhibition catalogue
 *La città di Leonardo, L'arte Contemporanea, Milano e
  Leonardo*, exhibition catalogue, Fondazione Stelline,
  Milan, Italy, Silvana Editoriale, Cinisello Balsamo (Mi)
 Painting codes. I codici della pittura, exhibition catalogue,
  Galleria Comunale d'Arte Contemporanea, Monfalcone,
  Italy
2005
 Tagliafierro, Marco, "Pietro Roccasalva si mette in scena,"
  La Repubblica, 21 May
 Changes of mind: transformation and belief, exhibition
  catalogue, Haunch of Venison, London
 Casavecchia, Barbara, Smarrelli, Marcello, "Pietro
  Roccasalva," *Follow your shadow—Premio Furla per
  l'arte/Young Italian Artist*, exhibition catalogue,
  Galleria d'Arte Moderna, Bologna, Fondazione Querini
  Stampalia, Venice, ED CHARTA, Milan, p. 72-73
 Generation of Art-10 anni alla FAR, (10 anni Fondazione
  Ratti), exhibition catalogue, Como, Charta, Milan
2004
 Rabottini, Alessandro, "Ouverture-Pietro Roccasalva,"
  Flash Art, no. 247, August-September, p. 116
 Paradiso-Inferno, exhibition catalogue, Lubrina Editore,
  Bergamo
2003
 Laubard, Charlotte, *Dissoi Logoi, Forse Italia*, exhibition
  catalogue, S.M.A.K., Stedelijk Museum voor Actuele
  Kunst, Ghent, Belgium, p. 54–56
 Great Expectations, exhibition catalogue, Fuori Uso,
  Pescara, Italy
 In Extremis, exhibition catalogue, Advanced Course in
  Visual Arts (with Giulio Paolini), Fondazione Ratti,
  Como, Charta, Milan
2002
 Rabottini, Alessandro, "Pietro Roccasalva," *La Ripro-
  riduzione*, exhibition catalogue, Istituto Nazionale per la
  Grafica e la Calcografia, Rome; Archivio di Stato, Turin,
  Italy, Silvana Editoriale, Cinisello Balsamo (Mi), p. 88-90

[p. 1] UNTITLED, 1992
Photograph, 22.4 x 17.8 cm; collection Sergio Bertola;
courtesy ZERO..., Milan

[p. 3] THE SKELETON KEY, 2006
Soft pastel on paper on forex, 58 x 48.5 cm; private
collection; courtesy ZERO..., Milan; photo Agostino Osio

[p. 4] MESSAGGERIE MUSICALI, 2002
Environment: wood, pastel on paper, laserprint mounted
on Plexiglas, digital animation; installation view at Church
San Francesco, Como (decommissioned); collection My
Private; courtesy ZERO..., Milan

[p. 5] UNTITLED, 2003
Pastel on paper on forex, 38 x 48 cm; collection Giorgio
Zaetta; courtesy ZERO..., Milan

[p. 6] INTELLIGENT ARTIFICE(R), 1999–2003
Oil on canvas on wood, 82 x 66 cm; collection My Private
Courtesy ZERO..., Milan

[p. 10] UNTITLED, 2003
Oil on canvas, 61 x 91 cm (detail); collection Giulio di
Gropello, Rome; courtesy Vistamare, Pescara

[p. 11] UNTITLED, 2006
Acrilyc and Indian ink on paper, 24 x 15 cm; collection
Giulio di Gropello, Rome; courtesy ZERO..., Milan; photo
Agostino Osio

[p. 12] FISHEYE, 2003
Environment: pyramid in lacquered wood, sculpture in
chrome plated metal, tablecloth, spongy carpet, oil on
canvas, chromate brass frame (detail); exhibition view
at Vistamare, Pescara; courtesy Vistamare, Pescara;
photo Mario Di Paolo

[p. 13] FISHEYE, 2003
Digital drawing, lambda print on aluminum, 35 x 45 cm

[p. 14] JOCKEY FULL OF BOURBON, 2003
Environment: soft pastel on paper on forex, microphone
pole, resin, painted feathers (detail); installation view at
Fuori Uso 2003, Ferrotel, Pescara; collection My Private
Courtesy ZERO..., Milan; photo Mario Di Paolo

[p. 15] JOCKEY FULL OF BOURBON, 2005
Color digital print, 37 x 30 cm; courtesy ZERO..., Milan

[p. 16] UNTITLED, 2007
Acrylic on paper on forex, 39 x 50 cm; detail of The Silent
Woman; private collection, Bolzano; courtesy ZERO..., Milan;
photo Agostino Osio

[p. 17] REX, 2004
Oven, resin, painted feathers, 80 x 65 x 60 cm; collection
Perna Foundation; courtesy ZERO..., Milan

[p. 18] UNTITLED, 1998
Soft pastel on paper on wood, 65 x 50 cm; private
Collection; courtesy Johnen+Schöttle, Cologne

[p. 19] O.H. SITUAZIONE D'OPERA IN QUATTRO STANZE, 2004
Environment: tableau vivant, digital animation, soft pastel
on paper on wood, oven, resin, painted feathers; exhibition
view at Viafarini, Milan; courtesy ZERO..., Milan; photo
Mario Di Paolo

[p. 21] THE OVAL PORTRAIT. A VENTRILOQUIST AT A BIRTHDAY
PARTY IN OCTOBER 1947, 2005
Tableau vivant, soft pastel on paper on panel, 91 x 150 cm;
installation view at Villa delle Rose, Bologna; courtesy
ZERO..., Milan; photo Ela Bialkowska

[p. 22–23] THE OVAL PORTRAIT. A VENTRILOQUIST AT A
BIRTHDAY PARTY IN OCTOBER 1947, 2005
Tableau vivant, soft pastel on paper on panel (detail),
91 x 150 cm; installation view at Villa delle Rose, Bologna;
courtesy ZERO..., Milan; photo Ela Bialkowska

[p. 25] THE OVAL PORTRAIT. A VENTRILOQUIST AT A BIRTHDAY
PARTY IN OCTOBER 1947, 2005
Oil on canvas, 32 x 26 cm; private collection; courtesy
ZERO..., Milan; photo Agostino Osio

[p. 26–27] THE GOOD WOMAN, 2005
Lacquered wood, painted clay sculpure, soft pastel on
paper on panel, 180 x 180 x 10 cm, Ø 40 cm, 48 x 38
cm; collection My Private; courtesy ZERO..., Milan; photo
Agostino Osio

[p. 27] UNTITLED, 2005
Acrylic on paper on forex, 35 x 50 cm; collection Edoardo
Gnemmi, Milan; courtesy ZERO..., Milan; photo Agostino Osio

[p. 28–29] JOCKEY FULL OF BOURBON II, 2006
Neon, resin and handpainted feathers, microphone pole,
acrylic on paper on forex, mirror, 290 x 680 x 580 cm;
installation view at Johnen+Schöttle, Cologne; courtesy
Johnen+Schöttle, Cologne

[p. 30] UNTITLED, 2006
Oil on paper on forex, 32 x 24 cm; collection Mitzi and
Warren Eisenberg, New York; courtesy ZERO..., Milan; photo
Agostino Osio

[p. 31] JOCKEY FULL OF BOURBON II, 2006
Neon, resin and handpainted feathers, microphone pole,
acrylic on paper on forex, mirror, 290 x 680 x 580 cm
(detail); installation view at Johnen+Schöttle, Cologne;
courtesy Johnen+Schöttle, Cologne

[p. 32] STUDY FOR Z, 2007
Tableau vivant; courtesy ZERO..., Milan; photo
Antonio Maniscalco

[p. 33] THE SILENT WOMAN, 2007
Wallpainting, lambda print on aluminum, acrylic on paper
on forex (detail), 425 x 360 cm, Ø 25 cm, 39 x 50 cm; private
collection, Bolzano; courtesy ZERO..., Milan

[p. 34–35] D'APRÈS LA TEMPESTA, 2006
Offset print on paper, fried rice ball, oil on canvas,
80 x 80 x 50 cm, Ø 30 cm, 83 x 73 cm; installation view
at Johnen+Schöttle, Cologne; courtesy Johnen+Schöttle,
Cologne

[p. 36] UNTITLED, 2003
Soft pastel on paper on forex, 45,5 x 31 cm; collection
My Private; courtesy ZERO..., Milan

[p. 37] STUDY FOR THE SKELETON KEY, 2007
Acrilyc on paper mounted on canvas, 13 x 19 cm; collection
Gaby and Wilhelm Schürmann, Herzogenrath; courtesy
ZERO..., Milan

[p. 38] UNTITLED, 2002
Tableau vivant; courtesy ZERO..., Milan

[p. 39] D'APRÈS LA TEMPESTA, 2006
Offset print on paper, fried rice ball, oil on canvas;
installation view at Johnen+Schöttle, Cologne; courtesy
Johnen+Schöttle, Cologne

[p. 40] GIOCONDITÀ, 2002
Digital animation, 3'53" loop; courtesy ZERO..., Milan

[p. 41] FISHEYE, 2003
Environment: pyramid in lacquered wood, sculpture in
chrome plated metal, tablecloth, spongy carpet, oil on
canvas, chromate brass frame (detail); installation view at
Vistamare, Pescara; courtesy Vistamare, Pescara; photo
Mario Di Paolo

[p. 41] UNTITLED, 2005
Mixed media on paper, 9.5 x 14.5 cm; private collection;
courtesy ZERO..., Milan

[p. 42] Andrei Tarkovsky, Andrei Rublev, 1966
205', film still

[p. 44] UNTITLED, 2004
Mixed media on paper, 21 x 30 cm; private collection
Montebelluna

[p. 45] Exhibition view My Private #4, 2006, Ex Tempio
Metodista, Turin
Photo Luca Fregoso

[p. 46–47] L'ANIMALE POVERO DI MONDO, 2006
Painted wood, performance, Ø 400 cm; 12 hours; exhibition
view My Private #4, Ex Tempio Metodista, Turin; collection
My Private; photo Luca Fregoso

[p. 48–49] L'UOMO FORMATORE DI MONDO, 2006
Sinopia, performance, 180 x 248 cm; 24 hours: one day's
work of fresco; exhibition view My Private #4, Tempio
Metodista, Turin (decommissioned); collection My Private;
photo Luca Fregoso

[p. 50] VIOLET FISHEYE II, 2007
Digital animation, 3'00" loop; courtesy ZERO..., Milan

[p. 51–52] DE MORGEN, 2006 (detail)
Environment: floor drawing, varan, fried rice ball, digital
animation; Installation view at Hoet Bekaert Gallery,
Ghent; courtesy Hoet Bekaert Gallery, Ghent; collection My
Private—on permanent loan at MARTa Herford Museum

[p. 55] UNTITLED, 1999
    Graphite on paper, 23 x 33 cm; private Collection, London;
    courtesy ZERO…, Milan; photo Agostino Osio
[p. 56] Exhibition view *Truka*, 2007, art: concept, Paris
    Environment: soft pastel on paper on forex, steel, hair,
    masking tape, film (detail); collection Sandra e Giancarlo
    Bonollo, Italy; courtesy art: concept, Paris
[p. 57] THE SKELETON KEY II, 2007
    Soft pastel on paper on forex, 70 x 50 cm; collection
    Sandra e Giancarlo Bonollo, Italy; courtesy art: concept,
    Paris
[p. 58] CLINAMEN II, 2007
    Steel, hair, masking tape, 700 cm; Ø 70 cm; installation
    view at GAMeC, Bergamo; collection MUSEION, Bolzano;
    courtesy ZERO…, Milan; photo Antonio Maniscalco
[p. 59] Exhibition view *Truka*, 2007, GAMeC, Bergamo
    Environment: soft pastel on paper on forex, steel, hair,
    masking tape, film; collection MUSEION, Bolzano; courtesy
    ZERO…, Milan; photo Antonio Maniscalco
[p. 60] THE SKELETON KEY III, 2007
    Soft pastel on paper on forex,189 x147 cm; collection
    MUSEION, Bolzano; courtesy ZERO…, Milan; photo Antonio
    Maniscalco

This book was published on the occasion of the exhibition *Pietro Roccasalva: Truka* at GAMeC—Galleria d'Arte Moderna e Contemporanea di Bergamo, June 6–July 29, 2007.

THIS PUBLICATION HAS BEEN REALIZED WITH

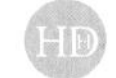

FONDAZIONE DAVIDE HALEVIM

ON THE INITIATIVE OF Edoardo Gnemmi

GAMEC – GALLERIA D'ARTE MODERNA E CONTEMPORANEA
Via S. Tomaso, 53
I-24121 Bergamo
www.gamec.it

ASSOCIAZIONE PER LA GALLERIA D'ARTE MODERNA
E CONTEMPORANEA DI BERGAMO – ONLUS

FOUNDING MEMBERS Comune di Bergamo, TenarisDalmine
MEMBERS Banca Popolare di Bergamo, Bonaldi
CONTRIBUTING MEMBERS Confindustria Bergamo
CHAIRMAN Mario Scaglia
TRUSTEES Giuseppe Calvi, Stefano Müller, Giovanni
Pandini, Armando Spajani
AUDITOR Anna Venier
BOARD OF EXPERTS Iwona Blazwick, Jan Hoet, Giorgio Verzotti
DIRECTOR Giacinto Di Pietrantonio
INSTITUTE DIRECTOR Maria Cristina Rodeschini Galati
CHIEF CURATOR Alessandro Rabottini
ASSOCIATE CURATOR Bruna Roccasalva
ASSISTANT CURATOR Sara Fumagalli
CINEMA CURATOR Sara Mazzocchi
GENERAL AFFAIRS Roberta Garibaldi
ADMINISTRATIVE MANAGER Marco Beolchi
COMMUNICATIONS Silvia Dondossola
PR Beatrice Ferrara
EDUCATIONAL DEPARTMENT COORDINATOR Giovanna
Brambilla Ranise
PROMOTION Clara Manella
ADMINISTRATIVE SUPPORT Rossella Della Monica, Claudio
Gamba, Lorella Grammatico, Ilaria Trussardi

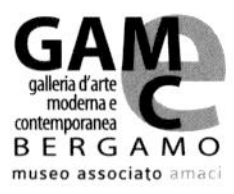

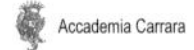

Associazione per la Galleria d'Arte Moderna e Contemporanea di Bergamo - onlus

FOUNDING MEMBERS

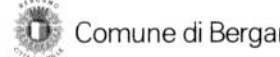

MEMBERS

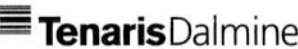

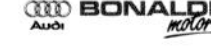

THIS PUBLICATION HAS BEEN POSSIBLE THANKS
TO THE GENEROUS SUPPORT FROM
art: concept, Paris
Johnen+Schöttle, Cologne/Berlin
ZERO…, Milan

WE WOULD ALSO LIKE TO THANK
Olivier Antoine, Delphine Bekaert, Barbara Casavecchia,
Claudia Ciaccio, Alice Conconi, Vincenzo de Bellis,
Anna Daneri, Greta Di Martino, Giacinto Di Pietrantonio,
Jan Hoet Jr., Jörg Johnen, Paola Manfrin, Markus
Mascher, Pierluigi Mazzari, Gianmarco Pozzoli, Giorgio
Roccasalva, Bruna Roccasalva, Giovanni Scivoletto, Antonio
Scoccimarro, Barry Schwabsky, Paolo Zani

PUBLICATION

EDITOR Alessandro Rabottini
TEXTS Edoardo Gnemmi, Alessandro Rabottini, Pietro
Roccasalva, Barry Schwabsky
EDITORIAL COORDINATION Birte Theiler
EDITING AND PROOFREADING Clare Manchester
TRANSLATIONS Anne Ruzzante
DESIGN no-do
COVER *Intelligent Artifice(r)*, 1999–2003
COLOUR STAMPA AND PRINT Musumeci S.p.a. (Aosta)
TYPEFACE Hermes Sans

Printed in Europe

PUBLISHED BY
JRP|Ringier
Letzigraben 134
CH-8047 Zurich
Tel +41 (0) 43 311 27 50
Fax +41 (0) 43 311 27 51
www.jrp-ringier.com
info@jrp-ringier.com

ISBN 978-3-905770-97-1

ALSO AVAILABLE
Italian edition: ISBN 978-3-905829-19-8

JRP|Ringier books are available internationally at selected
bookstores and from the following distribution partners:

SWITZERLAND
Buch 2000, AVA Verlagsauslieferung AG, Centralweg 16,
CH-8910 Affoltern a.A., buch2000@ava.ch, www.ava.ch

FRANCE
Les Presses du réel, 16 rue Quentin, F-21000 Dijon,
info@lespressesdureel.com, www.lespressesdureel.com

GERMANY AND AUSTRIA
Vice Versa Vertrieb, Immanuelkirchstrasse 12,
D-10405 Berlin, info@vice-versa-vertrieb.de, www.vice-
versa-vertrieb.de

UK AND OTHER EUROPEAN COUNTRIES
Cornerhouse Publications, 70 Oxford Street,
UK-Manchester M1 5NH, publications@cornerhouse.org,
www.cornerhouse.org/books

USA, CANADA, ASIA, AND AUSTRALIA
D.A.P./Distributed Art Publishers, 155 Sixth Avenue,
2nd Floor, USA-New York, NY 10013, dap@dapinc.com,
www.artbook.com

For a list of our partner bookshops or for any general
questions, please contact JRP|Ringier directly at
info@jrp-ringier.com, or visit our homepage www.jrp-ringier.com
for further information about our program.